Contents

Owning Racehorses
What It's *Really* Like

Owning Racehorses
What It's *Really* Like

David Byrne
with Lesley Bootiman

Scribblers 2 Ltd

Pubished by:
Scribblers 2 Ltd
Coombs End Farmhouse
Old Sodbury
South Glos. BS37 6SQ

CIP data:
A catalogue record for this book is available
from the British Library
ISBN 0-9548713-0-8

Designed and produced by John Elliott
Cover design by Steve Goodfield
Text set in Adobe Bembo

Printed by Alden Group Ltd
Osney Mead
Oxford OX2 0EF

To our mothers, Eleri and Sheila, each 87-years young and regular punters both.

The Authors

David Byrne and Lesley Bootiman in the winners' enclosure at Chepstow.

Acknowledgements

My special thanks go to the owners who appear in these pages. Jean Broadhurst, Robert Lester, Jim Lewis, Andy Stewart and Terry Warner all gave of their time and hospitality with remarkable generosity.

Five other people deserve special mention.

Terry Mountford is not only our racing partner and therefore has shared in the financial and emotional burdens of some of the horses who figure in these pages, but he has also proved to be an invaluable provider of photographs, an assiduous checker of facts and 'all-round' encourager.

My wife, Lesley, ('Mrs Byrne' in the book) has shared in all the financial and emotional burdens with regard to the horses. She has also provided support and encouragement throughout the project which goes way beyond the chapter and short story which are rightly acknowledged in her professional name.

Sadie Ryan at the Racehorse Owners' Association, was more than helpful. Steve Goodfield has been our business partner and a friend seemingly forever. This book bears his imprint. John Elliott has also been a true friend for many years, proving his good sense and judgement time and again.

There are two other groups who deserve special mention. First, all the trainers and their wives, stable staff, jockeys and their agents, who appear in these pages.

And last but certainly not least, the horses whose character, honesty and courage stir mine – and many other people's – souls.

The Horses

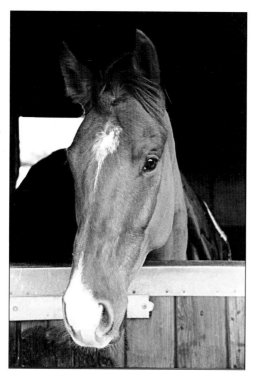

Gloster Gunner (top left), Jessie MacDougall (above), Burwood Breeze (below) and Klondike Charger (bottom left © Les Hurley).

Introduction

'Any man whose love of horses is stronger than his
fear of being an absurdity is all right by me'
Thomas Findley, Canadian writer.

'The profession of book writing makes horse racing
seem like a solid, stable business'
John Steinbeck, American writer

I suspect every owner, including the ones featured in this
book - plus all trainers, jockeys, stable staff and punters
everywhere - would say a loud 'hear, hear' to the first
quotation. If you want to present an image to the world as
a man or woman who is never wrong or you can't stand
being made to look a fool, keep away from horses.

As to the second, well, I have particular reason for saying
my own personal 'hear, hear' to Mr Steinbeck.

In 2001, after about ten years as an owner, and surprised
at how few books had been written about actually owning
horses, I decided to keep a diary. I would tell the truth about
what happened, not in the winners' enclosures at
Cheltenham or Aintree but in more modest surroundings -
the places where most owners enjoy their rare successes and
much more frequent disappointments.

To take Mr Findley's point, I would not just accept the
absurdity but I would tell it like it is. Unvarnished but I
hope with the odd smile, I would lay bare what really
happened to the seven horses in training in which I then

had an interest. I would explain what life was like with trainers, jockeys and co-owners, telling the truth about the costs and even letting light into the hitherto murky darkness of my gambling.

My book, my very first, was called *You Just Never Know*. I was naturally delighted when at only the fourth attempt – a much quicker rate than the average – the book was accepted by a publisher. And one, what's more, who specialised in books about sport and had handled the autobiographies of the tennis star, Pat Cash; England scrum half, Austin Healey; as well as a big seller, the memoirs of racing bad boy, Graham Bradley.

The book was planned to be launched alongside *Out of the Shadows*, jockey Richard Johnson's story and being published by the same firm. Somehow, in ways which were never fully explained, some of his stardust would sprinkle down on to my rather more ample shoulders.

To cut the story short, suffice it to say the firm went into liquidation just as, three months late from the printers, my book was arriving at the bookshops as they were closing their doors for Christmas. So having laid the love and absurdity bare – and received sympathetic looks from friends who'd read the book but who didn't share the passion – the words of Mr Steinbeck about the risks of book writing had come to pass.

The last I heard Richard Johnson was suing to try and get back £60,000 in unpaid royalties. For myself, deeply disappointed and having received not a penny and what's more after wasting money on lawyers, I decided 'enough'. It was one of those things. The book did get to some major bookshops and was available on the internet but had been launched with all the fanfare that only trumpeters without lungs could achieve (a set of circumstances, incidentally, some of us believe would improve the pre-race rituals at the tracks which come under Sir Stan Clarke's banner).

Far worse things occur ... but privately I ground my

teeth at any mention of *the book*. Then a strange thing happened. People started coming up to me at the races, saying how much they had enjoyed it.

With my name in the racecard as an owner - plus the book had a large picture of my ugly mug on the front cover - I was not hard to spot. Complete strangers - including owner Andy Stewart, one of the five featured in this book - picked me out to thank me for telling it like it was. Jim Lewis, the now legendary owner of Best Mate and Edredon Bleu - and another of the five featured here - was kind enough to say it was an 'excellent read' (which was nice) and that 'anyone even thinking of getting involved in racing should read it and keep it as handbook' (which for me was even nicer).

Perhaps the most remarkable was the very sweet lady at Stratford who without any preliminaries walked up to me and said: 'You're David Byrne aren't you? You're the reason I've got a racehorse.' Now there's a responsibility to place on a man's shoulders. It transpired that she'd wanted to have a horse, but she wanted her husband to understand what they were getting into. She'd insisted he read the book and even then he agreed! I have a funny suspicion that decision was rather more to do with true love than my book, but there it is.

Then a friend, a publisher of the non-sporting variety, hearing what had happened said he would be happy to re-publish it as it stood. I said no - but I would very much like to do it again.

It would be the all-new adventures of the four horses who now make up the Byrne string - plus this time it would feature portraits of five very different owners but ones who by a variety of routes had made it into the premier league of the jumping game. So this book is about the love - and the absurdity - at a number of different levels.

One of the questions you are always being asked as an owner is : 'Do you make money at it?' Certainly the author never has – and only one of the five other featured owners has done so. Of the two already mentioned, Andy Stewart – who with his wife owns Cenkos and a dozen more – says simply you can't expect to make money from a hobby; and Jim Lewis, with three Gold Cups on the sideboard, says he's pretty much put all his considerable winnings back into the sport.

Of the others, certainly not Terry Warner, who owns Rooster Booster and 14 others and has had horses for over forty years. 'I did the year we won the Champion Hurdle. But that was the first and only time.' Nor Jean Broadhurst who shares Upgrade and Westender and eight more and who says that if owners are even a bit in front, they're doing well.

The exception is Bob Lester, the owner of the Cheltenham long distance hurdle winner, Iris's Gift. But in case you think this Cheshire publican has learnt a trick which the others – all hard-headed and successful business people – have missed, remember two things.

First, this is a man whose £5,000 purchase had already won him around £300,000 and the horse is only a seven-year-old. But second, he has turned down several offers of over a million pounds for his five grand gelding. After that fact, don't anybody tell me that Bob Lester is in this for the money, nor that the love and absurdity is any different for him than the others.

David Byrne
Gloucestershire
June 2004

Chapter 1

Owning Horses

For my money, to see horses racing is one of the great sights. The creatures have a grace and splendour which artists have struggled to capture ever since our ancestors first decided to cheer up their cave walls. And it's not just the equines - a day at the races involves meeting as wide a range of people as you are likely to encounter anywhere. Add to all that, the variety of racecourses, each with its own character, then throw in the spice of gambling and you have a mixture which many of us find hard to beat no matter how many times we try it.

That's the reason people go racing in their millions and long may it continue. The simple thrill of shouting home *your* horse, chosen from racecard or form book or even by pin or because of a simple liking for the name, can be one of life's great, simple pleasures. After all, if that particular fancy fails to deliver, don't worry; there will be another race along in half an hour or so and provided the purse or wallet can stand it, you can have another go.

There are still days when, like most of the other owners featured, I head off to the races with none of my horses running and am more than happy to be just another punter, enjoying a day out with no concerns or responsibilities other than to enjoy the day. Of course a couple of winners helps, but the spectacle and competition will engage me even when all the money has gone down a strictly one-way street - from my pocket straight to the bookies.

For me it remains a sure-fire way of forgetting for a few

hours whatever cares and worries are currently finding space on my personal memo board. And after all, if we hadn't enjoyed the experience of being a racegoer plain and simple why would we have taken the next step and become owners?

There is no getting round the fact that once you pass through the door marked 'Owner' you enter a somewhat different arena. Of course the plus side is that you hope to find yourself shouting home not just *your* horse, picked from a racecard on the basis of whim or detailed research – but YOUR horse, the one with whom your name is inextricably linked and which carries your colours and your hopes.

Of course to shout that horse home into first place is what you want. That is a terrific experience, a 'high' which takes some beating. Not quite so good but still really something is cheering on your horse when he or she has honestly given of their best, even when they don't make the frame. You know, even if nobody else does, that next time will be different ...

The other side of the coin is the responsibility that ownership brings. You worry about the animal's well being away from the track and safety once it's there. Relationships with trainers and jockeys matter and of course there's the no small matter of the hideous expense of it all. So instead of the carefree punter at the racetrack simply enjoying a day out, you arrive consumed with concerns about minuscule changes to the going, thoughts about the wisdom of tactics and jockey riding styles, and bracing yourself for the stomach-churning minutes when the race actually starts.

And of course once you penetrate racing's attractive surface, inevitably a rather different, more complex world comes into view. Racing is big business and the politics of the sport, it has to be said, are not for the faint-hearted. The competing interests of bookmakers, racecourses, television companies, owners, sponsors, trainers and jockeys can sometimes make the rough old trade of ordinary politics seem, by comparison, pretty straightforward.

Why that should be so I will leave others to explain but what is for sure is that in many ways British racing, despite or because of the competing interest groups, is in a pretty healthy state. In 2003, according to the British Horseracing Board, six million people went racing while another set of figures tell us that about five hundred million worldwide watched British racing on television.

The figure of six million racegoers (making it the nation's second biggest spectator sport) is all the more remarkable when you consider that it is the best figure for half a century and when you also allow that in 2000 the total was 5.1 million.

Those racegoers have 59 racecourses in Britain to choose from, including two in Northern Ireland, which between them stage nearly 1,350 race days, consisting of almost 8,500 races, every year.

It makes for a serious industry. About 60,000 people work in racing and breeding (that's about one in eight of all agricultural workers) and there are another 40,000 people employed in the betting industry. They deal with the £8 billion which is bet off course every year, most of it in the 8,500 licensed betting shops scattered across the country.

Horse racing remains the most important single factor in betting, helping to produce around two thirds of the bookie's profits. The Government does o.k. too, taking around £250 million a year in betting duty receipts and garnering another £150 million from the racing and breeding industry's activities.

And the focus for all this activity – the horse. There are around a million of them in the U.K. (with two million regular riders), living testimony of the adaptability of a creature whose days as the nation's workhorse are long done. Left to their own devices, incidentally, they will happily spend about three quarters of their time eating.

The story of another season - the author's first book which details what happens when you have a responsibility for at least part of a string of over 20 thoroughbreds. This book is still available and you will find details inside the back cover.

YOU JUST NEVER KNOW ...

A Racehorse Owner's Season

DAVID BYRNE

Of course it is the thoroughbred which is the focal point of racing. About 14,000 thoroughbred foals are born every year with only three in a hundred ever winning a race.

Oddly enough, the same figure - 14,000 - applies when

you count up the number of thoroughbreds currently in training in the U.K. Along with the horses come about 9,500 active registered owners (nearly 7,000 of them members of Racehorse Owners Association). Because of the various kinds of multiple ownerships – partnerships, syndicates, racing clubs etc - that owner figure swells to around 50,000 people with at least a finger in the ownership pie.

Bigger owners are the exception. One candidate for the Racehorse Owners' Association Executive committee in the spring of 2004, estimated that 95% of the organisation's registered owners had an interest in two horses or less.

An odd bunch these owners. Like the rest of the human race they come in all shapes, sizes and genders. The proportion who own and run businesses - or have done - would seem to me to be a lot higher than average. That no doubt has to do both with being able to afford it and also not being subject to the usual rules about taking time off so they can see their horses race.

But they are seriously odd in one respect. Most people who have built up businesses have emerged with a healthy respect for making a profit and a regard for the bottom line little short of religious. The odd part comes in the complete disregard of that principle when it comes to owning and running racehorses.

In the last chapter of this book you will find laid out my costs and returns for the season, plus the average costs for all racehorse owners. On the grounds that there have probably already been enough facts and figures in this chapter, let me add just one set more before moving on.

Those hard-headed businessmen and women who are owners are choosing - nobody makes them - to put their hard earned money into an activity where on average, taking both flat and jump racing into account, they can expect (according to the latest ROA figures produced in autumn 2003) to recover a fraction short of 24% of their costs. No, we are not talking net or gross profit here. This is the amount on average they can expect to get back of the money they have put in.

In simple terms for every £10 owners put in they can expect to get back on average £2.40. In other words, owners subsidise the sport to the tune of £7.60 for every £10 they spend.

It is generally accepted that overall, owners directly contribute around £250 million net to the £500 million it costs to stage British racing every year. That money, directly and indirectly, flows to the professionals who make their money from racing – the trainers, jockeys, bookies, racecourse operators and all the other people who may well love the sport but also make their livings from it.

Let me repeat, nobody makes us owners do it and both the number of horses in training and the number of owners is on the rise. But do spare a thought for a special group in all this and one of which I am a member – the jump horse owner.

On average on the flat, an owner can expect his horse to run 5.5 times a season. For the owner of a jumping horse the average is 3.5 times. That has a nasty effect on the costs. The jumping owner can expect to get back less than £2 of every £10 he puts in – £1.80 to be precise.

So how did I come to be a member of this band, a group who when naively asked: 'Do you make money from it?' can't decide whether to choke on hollow laughter or bank-statement induced tears?

Certainly my family history doesn't contain too many thoroughbreds in the conventional sense, pit ponies perhaps but not blue bloods. I was born in South Shields at the mouth of the Tyne in the cold winter of 1947, a town which then had seven working collieries and four shipyards and now has none.

The nearest most of us got to horse racing was singing the Geordie anthem, *Blaydon Races* which for anyone who finds the North-east dialect difficult is in fact all about going along the Scotswood Road (in Newcastle) to see the Blaydon (horse) Races. 'All the lads and lasses there, all with smiling faces, gannin' alang the Scotswood Road ...'

My father's death from TB when I was just five months old left my mother, aged 30, to bring up three children under the age of six. Not surprisingly, with no visible means of support in those days when the words social security had yet to enter common parlance, she didn't think involvement in the sport of Kings need figure too highly in our daily lives.

Clutching five O levels (two attempts) at the age of 17, I somehow managed to become a cub reporter on a local weekly paper. That led to a similar role on an evening newspaper and, after a few years, a job as a producer at the start of BBC Local Radio.

By the age of 24 I was in BBC telly, had met and married the understanding person who is still my wife, but there were no horses, until, that is, the day I went to Great Yarmouth for a programme we were making, in search of the then chairman of the Trainers' Federation.

I never did find him but I did fall in love (for the second time, I hasten to add) – with the racehorse. Yarmouth races may be a long way from the places where my dreams are now set but I can still remember seeing those gleaming creatures and the bright silks of the little men who rode them. I was hooked and have remained so since.

Of course, with two children and a mortgage to support, it was a distant love affair but in 1980 my wife and I had started our own communications business. From small acorns ... well not quite. Our business was never a giant oak but we did well and after about ten years we started to make profits enough to fund a half share in a hunter chaser.

He never did win - but undeterred my wife and I joined a syndicate and our horse did win three times. That led in time to a third share in an owning and breeding set-up.

There were more winners as well as part responsibility for more than 20 horses. Be warned: this owning business can be seriously addictive.

When the breeding operation was brought to an amicable end, we finished up with a half share in four home-bred horses plus two we owned ourselves. By the time this diary started two of the home breds were happily doing things other than racing.

The ups and downs of life with the remaining four horses, two wholly-owned and two part-owned, form the basis of my owner's diary.

Chapter 2

Miss Jean Broadhurst – the Gaffer

The next time anyone says to you that our modern world is a dull old place because there aren't any 'characters' any more, tell them to get themselves down to Bordesley Green in Birmingham. There, in Doris Road, in a part of the city which is very industrial and very Birmingham, they'll find the head office of European Steel Sheets. After that, it shouldn't take too long for them to come across the boss of that business, one Miss Jean Broadhurst.

It is just possible, if they're racing fans, that they might even recognise her from the telly. Miss Broadhurst (never Ms) is the owner of, among others, Upgrade, who won the Triumph Hurdle and quite a few since. She is the lady with the enormous hats and the even bigger glasses who makes quite a show of her appreciation of the efforts of winning jockeys. She covers them in more lipstick than is usually seen about their persons - at least during their normal working hours. And this even among a group of chaps known to slip into a pair of ladies tights under their breeches at the sight of a thermometer dropping.

She's famous too for her propensity for getting down on the rails to cheer her horses home and woe betide anyone who dares to encourage any other runner in the race. And if her horse does win she makes no effort to hide her feelings. I know one fellow-owner who was with her when Upgrade won the Triumph in 1998. He says his lips are still recovering.

I come from a very grass roots family where people kiss and hug when they're pleased with each other. At the races, when I first did it, they looked at me as if I was mad. But I don't give a damn. I want to show everybody how wonderful it is. Why not? I'm very comfy with my own people, my own sort. Westender ran on the flat at the Royal Ascot meeting. I thought 'Not for me. Let's get back to the sticks.' I like National Hunt and getting on the rails and having a good shout and nobody too bothered about what they're going to say.

Jean Broadhurst and her partner of 24 years, Matt Archer, have ten horses in training with Martin Pipe. It was Mr Archer who first owned horses and she 'sort of followed about ten years ago.' A question about which horses are jointly and which ones individually owned produces a response which is repeated a number of times in the course of our conversation. 'That's for me to know – and for you to wonder' she replies, fixing me with what can only be called a steely gaze.

On the subject of Martin Pipe she is a lot more forthcoming:

Martin is the best. He just is. There are so many facets that make him so good as to be untrue. He's not a pushover, he's not an easy man so that you can say what you like. He runs it his way. That's the way it should be – like I run my business. Some owners resent it but at the end of the day if you're going with Martin Pipe you have to know he's in charge. He decides who rides, where the horse runs. How can you tell the best what to do? It seems a bit pointless.

Until five years ago the horses were with Nigel Twiston-Davies.

We're stickers we are. It's a big thing to change your trainer. He's a good lad, a first class trainer who does well on the big occasion. We're still mates with Nigel but we moved when there was that talk about his closing down.

We're sitting talking in the accounts office of her

company. Her office, which is literally covered wall-to-wall with photographs of her racing triumphs, is being used for a meeting. Today there are no big hats. She has over a hundred made by the Queen's hat-maker and she has a lady who looks after them and the race day special outfits. She doesn't need them to cut a striking figure. Instead this imposing woman is allowing her spiky white blonde hair full rein and she's wearing a pair of spectacles that really are the size of two television screens. Then there's her voice. She can clearly rasp and roar with the best of them and all in tones as unmistakably Birmingham as the steel she sells.

Here she is not Miss Jean Broadhurst, racehorse owner, she is known simply and universally as 'The Gaffer.' In the next door office are 'the lads' - her sales team whose job it is to shift the steel the Gaffer has bought from suppliers. And the horses, they're 'the boys'. She explains how she and Matt Archer share a working routine which would not suit every couple.

Her partner is Birmingham's 'Mr Fruit and Veg'. He leaves their home at Lapworth in Warwickshire at around 1 a.m. every day and returns about 12 hours later having sorted the city's greengrocery needs. Jean Broadhurst is by comparison with him a late riser - but only with him. She leaves home every day at 4.30 a.m. and is in her office by 5.30. There she stays until around 5.30 p.m. every weekday. She is now 62. 'I used to work until around 8 o'clock every evening but I decided when I was 60 not to do that any more.' But there are no plans to reduce the hours any further.

I have the same view as Lord Lew Grade. He said the one word which should be taken out of the English dictionary is 'retirement'. The thought is terrifying. It makes people grow old and they become second-class citizens - and that I don't want to be. I've been here in Birmingham forever and I've got my street cred. I like it here and I like working. I spend my days dealing with suppliers - and talking to people about the horses which takes up half the day.

The horses are an important part in the Gaffer's life - but not the most important part. She inherited what was then a very small business from her much-revered father nearly forty years ago and building it up and running it have been the main focus of her life. But she says you can't underestimate the value of the horses in advertising her business.

Saatchi and Saatchi couldn't have done a better job. The horses have been absolutely marvellous for us. All the time people ring about the horses. I say to the lads, my sales team, talk about the horses - and get the deal. Customers will watch them on the telly and put some money on. Some of our big wins, I think just about everybody in the Midlands seems to have had a hundred quid on.

The company buys and sells steel with the end customers the hundreds of companies who have made the Midlands synonymous with metal bashing. At first when I try to gauge the company's size and success, I meet with another steely gaze and another 'For me to know and you to wonder.' But later she relents and tells me that the two companies she owns, together made over £2 million last year - 'not bad from somebody who's come out of the gutter' - and there are around 60 employees at two main sites.

On the side of the lorries which transport the steel, the horses play a prominent part. The logo in which they feature is changed every year and a new design has just been agreed.

> This one will feature a horse jumping over a fence. It'll be quite different from the one we've got now.
>
> You've got to keep people's interest. If you see the same old thing eventually you don't even notice it - but if you can get them to say 'Blimey what 's she got on there now?' you're getting somewhere.

But there are strict rules about when the Gaffer goes racing. Weekends she'll travel anywhere to see them run. But weekdays – with very, very rare exceptions - are out.

> I can't go in the week - what would my customers do? You have to be at your post. If you miss an offer, they're not going to wait for you to get back. It's a bit of an opportunistic business and you're doing deals virtually all the time. It's very hard work and you've got to be a bit tough with everybody. But since when was business for the weak at heart?

Even if she can't leave the office she makes sure she follows her horses' every move.

> I feel terrible when the horses run. I get so nervous. Before Westender ran in the Champion Hurdle, I got so nervous my

heart was missing a beat. The lads said to me 'It's about the only thing that'll make you like that, Gaffer.' And I said: 'You'd better believe it.'

This is a tough game for a woman. I have had to fight to get acceptance - I still do. When have you chaps ever given us girls credit for anything? All you think is that we should be at home baking cakes. Girls don't want to do that any more and I don't blame them. I was just a bit in front of the others.

I've learned to be frightened of no man. I'd face the whole British Army if I had to.

In a whole lot of ways Jean Broadhurst is anything but your average owner. She's never married, she doesn't smoke, she doesn't gamble, she never takes a holiday – 'why would I want to lie on a beach and get fried like a chip?' - and she doesn't drink. What, not even a glass of champagne after a big win? The steely gaze melts - and becomes simply contemptuous. 'Who needs it? I've been a teetotaller all my life. Swigging champagne - that's very 1960s that is. Very passé.'

She also has very clear views about the responsibilities of owners once their horses' racing days are over.

When you buy a racehorse you don't just buy them for the years they can race. You've got to look after them. I know what you're going to say - not everybody can do that because they haven't got the land. Those people should put up bonds so that if they can't do it they can get some horse centre to do it for them.

I've got all the ones that have raced for me at home. They're my responsibility, you've got to look after them. Some people buy them and then throw them out. And then you've got people like me who take them in.

In the thirty acres around her home, she has twelve of her own retired racehorses - and another six rescue cases. The oldest is 'Sid', at 29 a long retiree whose racing name was, believe it or not, Deadly Going. At 4 a.m. each day she helps the couple who look after them with feeding Sid and the others before setting off to work.

And it's not just the retired and the rescued who get special attention. While I was with her a fax came in from the Pipe yard thanking her for around forty boxes each of carrots and apples arranged through Mr Archer. From, it said, Arlas, Gone Far, Neutron, Samsaam, Sixo, Team Tassel, Westender, Upgrade, Villa and Your So Cool - obviously the ten horses who make up the Broadhurst/Archer string. It was addressed simply to 'Mom'.

So where and how does she buy her horses? For the third time I am advised that's for her to know and me to wonder and it's followed by an emphatic 'My game's buying and selling steel.' But again she relents. 'Sometimes Martin Pipe suggests a horse. It depends. I've learnt by trial and error.' She very nearly bought Rooster Booster. Was around £60,000 what she spends on average on a horse?

> Sometimes less, sometimes more. We bought Ocean Hawk, who won everything including the Long Walk hurdle, for a song. Then you buy dearer ones and you struggle with them. There's no guarantees.

Of course there've been bad days as well as good. Old Californian was killed at the track as was Kerawi. They were both brought back to Warwickshire to be buried.

> It's awful, very distressing. But you have to remember it's not the owner's fault. Life is full of ups and downs. We've had a lot of tragedy in our family - I buried my Mum and my brother-in-law in the same week. We coped. In life you've got to cope - it tests you as a person, shows what you're made of. And I'm made of good old Birmingham steel. Remember, when you cry, you cry alone. You've got to get back up.

This from a woman who had her own near ten-year battle with cancer, a period now long gone. 'Racing's a real tonic - much better than that chemo they gave me when I had that cancer of the glands.'

What about her ambitions? 'I'd like to win them all - the Cheltenham Gold Cup particularly. I tell Martin 'I want one of those Gold Cups Jim Lewis has got. He always laughs. I tell you what, that Jim Lewis is a lovely man and that Best Mate is a staggering horse.'

She reckons Upgrade to be the best horse she has had.

He's a character. He won a lot of good races and then hit a bad spell. I said to Martin 'We all have bad spells.' I said I'd had plenty. I said he would pick himself back up. And he has. Westender, he's seven now, he's a lovely horse, one for the future. But you know horses aren't so unlike you and me. They might have a good day today or they might not. He hasn't really fired this last season - but he will. You've got to look after them.

And she has another rule. 'Your horse can run well and not even get a place. I make as much fuss of them then as I do when they win.'

Overall how would she sum up the season just gone? 'Not as good as last season - or the season before. But I've just bought some youngsters. It takes time for them to come through.' A question about whether or not she made money from her racing ownership brought the now familiar riposte as well as:

If owners are a bit in front, they're doing well. But for me, the horses have made many thousands for my company.

And then it was time to go. I'd been warned in advance that if she didn't like me I'd be out the door in five minutes. But she'd talked for well over an hour and, despite the odd steely gaze, I'd survived. Now it was time for her to get back to what she knows and loves best, buying and selling steel - and talking about the horses.

As I stood up to leave she suddenly planted a big smacking kiss on my cheek. 'I like you' she said.

I had two immediate thoughts. One, this was definitely the nearest I will ever get to being a winning jockey.

And two? That the feeling was mutual.

Chapter
3

David's Diary 1

OCTOBER 4

This is a day which still sends a shiver down my increasingly aged spine. Today we've jump racing at Chepstow, *The Capital Racecourse of Wales* as it is now billed ('Not a lot of competition in that race' as a trainer might well say to a hopeful owner). For me – and plenty like me – this is the day the *proper* National Hunt season gets under way.

Please don't get me wrong – summer jumping, as this diary will show, has provided some smashing moments. But when dreams are dreamt it's the winter game centre stage every time. Chepstow's October meeting is the one which to my mind sees the start of a process which will lead to the splendours of Cheltenham in March and the thrills of Aintree in April.

For the first time today we shall see in serious races some of the contenders whose owners, trainers and jockeys fervently hope will be involved when planned push comes to serious shove in about six months time. For about the last 20 years this early October meeting has been a fixture in my diary – but this year it is different. We have a runner.

The *we* in this case is my wife Lesley and our racing partners, Terry and Lilian, who share two horses and call ourselves *Four for Fun*. Previously, when many more horses were involved, we were two thirds of a partnership called *Three of a Kind*. No less than 23 horses came under that banner and today's runner Jessie MacDougall was one product of our breeding operation.

Klondike Charger with Andrew Thornton aboard is led in by Mrs Byrne and Ollie Dayman after winning at Fontwell for the second time in five days (Photo © Connors Photography).

The Trainers:

Above: The Doc and Mrs Doc – Philip and Teresa Pritchard. As well as rider and trainer, the Doc is a G.P. and racecourse doctor plus house and horsebox builder. Mrs Doc helps run the yard, is a horse and human chiropractor and the mother of two young sons.

Left: *Trainer Tom* – Tom George whose yard notched up a record total of 50 winners in 2004.

35

Strange the way the less horses we have, the greater the number we have in the name. Could it be that coming soon will be *Five Go Broke*?

Jessie, it has to be said, is not running in one of the premier races on the card - but it is by no means impossible that a horse doing well in the Bideem Juvenile Novices' Hurdle (class D) for three-year-olds could find itself in the babies' championship race at Cheltenham, a contest otherwise known as the Triumph Hurdle.

Jessie is an almost blue black filly trained not far from Chepstow by David Evans (P.D. Evans in the racecard) at Pandy near Abergavenny. Her father (the 'by' part of the breeding equation) is Overbury, a winner of group races on the flat.

She ran five times for us as a two-year-old last season, amazing nobody more than her trainer, jockey and owners by winning her very first visit to the track at Haydock Park. It was downhill from there, four more runs producing nothing better than a fourth in a twelve-runner seller.

This season - which in her case started deliberately late in August - has been a bit more consistently hopeful. Six runs, all on the flat on firm or good to firm ground, have produced a third and two fourths in big fields.

She is one of nine runners and, like four others, she has never run over hurdles before. Trainer Evans is not a man to mince his words. Jessie has run eleven times on the flat and in his straight-talking way he has made it clear that on the flat she is nothing to write home about, a bit above selling class but not much. Will win races for us, should have some fun - but don't get your hopes up too high.

All four owners are northerners, two each from the North-east and North-west - traditionally believers in the merits of plain speaking. In Mr P.D. Evans we have certainly met at least our equal. We have become used over the two seasons he has trained our horse to any suggestion by us of even mild enthusiasm about Jessie's future performance receiving Trainer Evans's all purpose put down: 'Just remember, she's modest.'

The fact that she wasn't going to set the world on fire as a flat horse caused this part-owner less disappointment than you might imagine. Whisper it in the dark at midnight, but compared with jump racing I agree with the man who said about the sport on the level: 'Flat – and rather boring.'

So in mapping out some kind of a plan for Jessie's season there was one voice in particular keen to see how Jessie would fare 'over the sticks'. That was the reason for her deliberately late reappearance. We would see how she went on the flat but have the option to try her over hurdles, hopefully on easier ground.

As well as Evans the Trainer, there is also Evans the Jockey - the trainer's son. What's more, Evans junior is a jump jockey with a three pound allowance (and in my opinion definitely one of the younger jockeys to watch). And it was to him Evans senior turned when the time came to introduce Jessie to hurdles over his training obstacles.

We expected a continuation of the 'Don't get your hopes up - remember she's only modest' theme when we asked how things had gone. Imagine our surprise then when the report came back after the first training session in just one word. Jessie had been, said Evans the Trainer, 'brilliant'. And what's more, after six training sessions 'bloody brilliant'. Because of the source it was more than a bit like Victor Meldrew suddenly bursting into 'Oh What a Beautiful Morning'.

And it was, as it happens, a very pleasant morning when Terry and friend came to collect me for the 20 minute run from my home to the track. The lady partners – in every sense – had opted to come later in time to catch Jessie's race while the males were keen to catch every minute of all the other action.

Weather, I have to warn all prospective owners, will come to figure very large in your life. Years ago I used to scorn my dear old, long-dead stepfather because of his very English obsession with the weather.

Perhaps he's looking down with a wry smile on a stepson who has now become an addict of the BBC Weather site on the internet, which gives five day forecasts for individual towns. Then, of course, you have to keep track of the forecasts on radio and television and in the newspapers. Next you wear out the buttons on your remote control getting the Racecourse Association going updates on BBC 2 (teletext channel 690 for the uninitiated). All of that information comes together when I ring the seemingly ever-patient clerks of the courses and press them not to tell me the current ground conditions but what they expect on race day.

After our long hot summer, clerks of the course have a problem as to how much to water. Over the years, courses get reputations for how much water they use or don't use. Chepstow has a reputation of being liberal with the tap-turning. Today's official 'good to firm ground' would, it has been suggested to us, be 'good' anywhere else.

In the car it takes about 30 seconds for Terry and myself to get to the weather and going issue. Promised showers have failed to materialise but we have been assured by the trainer that she will be o.k. although more cut would help. You can often tell from a horse's action – the way they move across the ground – what they prefer. When there is a roundness in the action it usually means something softish would be best. Jessie, who has performed reasonably well on the level on today's ground, has that characteristic – but no 'good to soft' conditions have been available for months for us or anyone else.

Terry's pal, no doubt bored rigid by the ability of his fellow travellers to discuss weather from now until the hereafter (or as Terry would say – long enough 'to put a glass eye to sleep') asks what instructions we will give to the jockey, Trainer Evans being with a horse at the big Cambridgeshire meeting at Newmarket.

Evans the Jockey, whose work on the training gallops has led to the 'brilliant' summation, is unavailable to us having fractured a finger. In his place we have Timmy Murphy, a rider whose career took quite a tumble after being found guilty of misbehaving (to put it politely) on a flight back from Japan. The subsequent jail sentence can't have been fun and cost him his retainer with the Paul Nicholls yard.

The instructions, I said, would be easy. Would he please not have a drink before the race; could he confine his urinary efforts to the gents loo; not to stray into the lady jockeys' training room; oh yes, and would he mind wearing our racing colours and not those ones with the big arrows.

Our Four for Fun partners, Terry and Lilian Mountford.

Alright I got my laugh - but Murphy, who has a deserved reputation as an astute horseman who handles young horses particularly well, has performed miracles in re-establishing himself. He has foresworn the booze and been given a helping hand by many racing people who understand better than most the pressures these guys are under. Last season it was obvious that a genuine talent was back on track.

Chepstow was, and still is, one of my favourite courses. And not just because it is the closest jumping track to my home. I say *was* because it was here I first started to really get to know and love the jumping game. I say *is* because it is now part of Sir Stanley Clarke's racing empire, which now also takes in Newcastle, Sedgefield, Uttoxeter, Hereford, Stratford, Bath, Great Yarmouth, Brighton and Fontwell Park. And Sir Stan certainly believes in change.

Most of it has been for the good – but like a few more I know, about Chepstow we wonder. No matter, today, even though we would much prefer torrential rain to obscure the view, the whole scene looks lovely. Autumn-tinted leaves on the trees around the course add a special touch in the sunshine.

So to our race, the 4.05, the third of three rides for Timmy Murphy, that afternoon. 'How's the ground?' I ask in the parade ring. 'I'd say on the dead side' comes the answer. That means that there's no bounce to it, with no cut either. I ask if he had a chat with the trainer and he explains that because of the current dispute about the use of mobile phones in the weighing room he hasn't been able to have a word.

So I pass on the fruits of our trainer's thoughts – try and make sure she has a nice introduction to hurdle racing and try and lay her up in fourth or fifth place. I get a smile when I say that he must be sick of people giving those instructions about fourth or fifth place and then with my standard (alright superstitious) 'Good luck – and come back safe' he's in the saddle and I'm off to the bookies' ring.

I have already laid £25 e.w. on my account with Tote Credit (having rung earlier to check that my cheque had cleared and on being told that it had and I owed nothing got a laugh when I said that didn't happen too often).

There must have been more than 40 bookies in the ring that day. I would say no more than five would do each way. She was universally 25/1 win only. The best price I spotted was 12/1 each way and most were less than that. I laid £20 e.w. at twelves safe in the knowledge that I would get the near-universal 25/1 which would obviously be the starting price (as it proved) thanks to my credit bet. O.K. for me – but you can see where it leaves the average fiver each-way punter.

Some of my thoughts about bookies can be found elsewhere – but I must report the bizarre circumstances in which Terry laid his bet. He was standing next to William Hill's pitch on the rails which was showing 16/1 each way (more fool me, I had gone down the line in the main ring).

Terry, who has more accounts than Lloyds TSB, then used his mobile to ring William Hill and asked for their each way price. '25/1' he was told. Blinking at the William Hill board in front of him – still showing 16/1 – guess what, he laid the bet off-course. And what's more several minutes later, and unable to get a better price, he did the same thing again. Still 16/1 at the track – and 25/1 off-course.

The race itself proved to be a sight less bizarre than the events in the bookies' ring. Jessie ran well enough to finish 4th, around 20 lengths off the winner, Web Perceptions, ridden by one A.P. McCoy; with the second, Sunray, in the hands of R. Johnson. We looked to have a real chance, after the second last hurdle, of getting third place – but it was not to be.

After the end of the race there was immediately an unscheduled contest not on the racecard. It involved self and wife trying to get from the owners' and trainers' viewing balcony down to the winners' enclosure. The new owners' and trainers' bar was packed to the point of bursting (could it be that Chepstow are taking a lenient view for the moment because of the building work in the members area?) and I decided the only way we would get to have that precious word with the jockey when the horse and race are fresh in his mind was by hurdling the guy rope which separates the owners' and trainers' balcony from same in a next-door corporate hospitality box.

So hurdling and smiling (with a certain amount of determined clench in the smiles) and with one of the runners definitely carrying over weight, we parted the corporate guests, and fled down the stairs to the weighing room and so out to the track to the winners' enclosure.

When I said Jessie *ran* well enough I meant just that – the jumping was another matter. Ah, the difference between events at home and at the racecourse. As a clearly puzzled Timmy Murphy put it once he was out of the saddle. 'We would have been third if she had jumped the last - or any one of the others.'

She had stuttered and hesitated at just about every hurdle. Puzzlement rather than disappointment was clear in what the jockey told us. 'I tried squeezing her before a hurdle and then letting her sort it out but it just didn't seem to make any difference' said the jockey.

The trip, he said, was fine; she would prefer more cut but the hurdling was another matter. We heard from trainer Evans later that the travelling lad and he himself had had earache from the jockey about who had schooled the horse.

But trainer Evans was adamant - 'she's been well schooled, at pretty well racing pace, and she's never made a mistake.' And what was more: 'I am telling you she can do much better than that - she will win races.'

Hey ho, the horse is just three, she is learning and she had come fourth in a race for which we had been cautious about entering her because it looked hot. Of course third would have been better - those each ways at 25/1 would have paid out for a start - but with £250 appearance money to add to a fourth prize of £234 we have the jockey fee and the transport with a few quid left over.

The plan will be to keep her ticking over with perhaps another run on the flat - and then put her back over the obstacles towards the end of the month when 'surely we will have had some rain.' And also, perhaps, she will show more of her hurdling brilliance.

As always in racing, tomorrow is another day.

Opposite: Jessie MacDougall leaves the parade ring at Chepstow, Timmy Murphy in the saddle.

OCTOBER 5

The day dawned bright and sunny - chilly with it but the sunshine and blue skies promised warmer weather as the day went on. All of which I hoped boded well for the second equine member of our cast, one Klondike Charger

by official name - otherwise known (his stable name) as Colin and one of two horses the Byrnes own outright.

Now to say that Colin is a bit of a character is putting it mildly, the equivalent of saying that A.Hitler or J. Stalin weren't entirely nice people. According to my daughter, at whose yard he had spent the winter, he is simply 'the laziest horse in Britain'. He either walks (very slowly) or goes at full gallop - trot, canter or anything else in between being far too much effort for this fella.

He is also something of a freak, a three mile chaser who wants it minimum good to firm. And just to complete this character CV he is what is known in racing circles as a *monkey*, a horse with ability who does his damndest to avoid showing it. To be honest, he has reduced me to frustrated fury at his unpredictability and there have been times when it was as well no shot gun was easily to hand - but rather like a particularly difficult aunt you finish up rather admiring him for the way he deals with the world strictly on his terms.

On the plus side of the ledger, he is very popular with the stable staff. Colin causes no bother, is easy to handle and overall has more than a touch of the horizontal in his laid back attitude. He remains popular despite sometimes with no warning suddenly whipping round and depositing the rider in a heap. All part of the process of Colin making it plain that he does things differently.

The compensation comes when he has to jump an obstacle. On his day he jumps wonderfully well, often taking two or more lengths out of the opposition at each fence, fiddling and adjusting where others would fall. Whisper it - but the sight of him really taking a cut at his fences brings both admiration and pride of ownership to this particular breast.

Whisper it even more quietly, and with fingers firmly crossed - he has a terrific record, never falling once so far in 33 outings over wood and birch. He is also versatile, tackling (if that's not a too active word for Colin) anything from a bit over two to well over three miles while barely breaking sweat. We often look at him immediately after a race in the winners' enclosure or the unsaddling area and say that you can see that such has been the exertion in the race that he 'wouldn't even blow out a candle.'

Colin arrived in this world with the paperwork for his PhD thesis *Looking After Yourself* absolutely all in order and clasped firmly in his hoof. He clearly has plans to get the horse equivalent of the Nobel prize for the same subject before he is done.

Klondike Charger is American bred (the USA that appears in brackets in the newspaper and race card) on both his father' and mother's sides. His mother's name? Forever Waving.

So much for the plusses. Turning to the debit side, among the other characteristics to be dealt with are his dislike of large fields of fellow runners (in fact truth to tell I am not sure he is overly fond of his fellow equines, either as individuals or as a group) and even in small fields he has a specific objection to other horses' backsides. Now this could be a real plus but in Colin's case it manifests itself in a downing of tools if too many of them come into view as the other horses go past him.

Then there is the weather. If you could picture a horse wearing a large pair of sun glasses, comfortably stretched on his lounger, the book being *500 Ways to Take It Easy* and with a waiter serving up a large helping of hay (oats might indicate activity) you'd get the idea.

Even at home before a training canter if the wind blows and there's rain about Colin rounds his shoulders and makes it very plain that we can do what we want, but HE doesn't want to play. Surely anybody with even an iota of common sense would stay in the dry on a day like this!

I can remember when we had made the considerable journey to Sedgefield. After a sunny morning it started to

James Davies and
Klondike Charger at
Stratford
(Photo © Les Hurley).

rain just as the horsebox arrived. Three hours later it was still raining and, for September, not that warm. A deeply miserable Colin was produced in the parade ring. He looked for all the world as if he wanted to be anywhere except where he was and if he could, I think he would have cried. For reasons which could only be to do with deepest sympathy for the wretched creature before them, they awarded him best turned out, regarded by me and many others as the kiss of death. He then proceeded to run as if suicide offered the only hope.

And on top of all that, he is a wise old bird who can clearly count how many circuits make three. Some days twice past the winning post is more than enough thank you very much and he wants immediately to show the jockey the way to his horsebox and his hay where he would very much like to be left in solitary peace - IF YOU DON'T MIND.

Then there is one's mood on a given day. My father-in-law was a Northumbrian, a fisherman turned water bailiff who, I suspect, will be one of the last to speak with the authentic rolling 'r'of the English border counties. This, allied with a pipe clamped firmly between his teeth, made him not always the easiest chap to follow. He also had a fund of words which aren't too often heard. For instance in his world nothing was ever so simple as *posh*. Instead a pub or restaurant would be *scenty-bottle*. And Lionel Willam Bootiman, 'Silence' in the family - (don't ask), did not say: 'Greetings old bean - how are you?' but rather the much more penetrating 'how's your fettle?' Never mind your health, what's your mood.

Colin is a fettle horse if ever there was one. If the fettle is right he pricks his ears, the eyes are bright and he actually appears to have some interest in proceedings in the parade ring. If not, Colin is the one whose handler is half dragging the horse around, not a good omen for the three miles of steeplechase fences to come. Who knows, a few more like Colin and we could add to the letters that appear in race cards - BF for beaten favourite, D for Distance winner and so on. We could have Fg and Fb for Fettle good and Fettle bad.

It is no great surprise then to discover that Klondike Charger's father was one Crafty Prospector.

All in all, not exactly a punter's dream. My wife and self had bought him the previous season as an eight-year-old and in fairness his 'little ways' had not been kept from us.

Following a chance conversation with trainer Paul Nicholls at Hereford races, I'd gone to his yard near Shepton Mallett in Somerset. Colin's then owner had become disillusioned with his little ways and to be honest, I don't think the man who for the last two seasons has been giving Martin Pipe a real run for his money in the trainers' championship was exactly close to tears at the prospect of bidding Colin farewell. He was very straight about the horse's attitude and correctly predicted that 'he will win races for you.'

We paid £6,000 for him, a sizeable drop from the

£100,000 he had cost as an unraced yearling. His career on the flat had certainly not lived up to expectations.

Before he came to us he had run 28 times, winning a hurdle race and two chases. His exasperated previous owner had called enough when he was pulled up at Uttoxeter. Things did not get off to a fairy tale start for us either when the same thing happened when he ran for the first time in our blue and white stripes at Worcester.

Things improved from there as we got used to him and that season, in nine runs for us, he finished second four times – frustrating but keeping hope alive. In the process he had won around £7,000 in place money, enough to pay for his bed and board if not to cover the initial outlay.

This new summer jumping season had not started well. The first three runs were dismal and I started to wonder if he had gone sour. But a second at Stratford in early August had laid the ground for our best ever few days as owners. Not only did Colin win over three miles two furlongs at Fontwell Park on August 18 (with the commentator talking about his 'bravery' in winning by two-and-a half lengths – What? Colin? Surely some mistake) but knock me down with a crumpled betting slip, he did it again on August 22 – just five days later – this time over two miles and six.

On that day, on clouds nine and ten, my wife and I had accepted that it was impossible to get from the Fontwell 4.40 p.m. celebrations to Bath at 7.25 p.m. on a Bank Holiday weekend. There, the aforementioned Jessie MacDougall was making her seasonal reappearance. We would listen to the live commentary of that race on the phone as we drove our euphoric way home ('Two wins in five days – this doesn't happen to people like us').

Mrs Byrne was driving because unlike me she doesn't like champagne - a statement which somehow doesn't quite convey the gulf between us over that particular matter. But then infinity wouldn't quite measure it either.

'Shouldn't we pull over and listen?' she asked. 'Don't be

daft', says I, 'She's 50/1, it's her first run of the season - she hasn't a hope in hell.'

Two furlongs from home Jessie came like the proverbial bat out of hell. She finished by far the fastest to take third place – and if the race had been just 100 yards further… At exactly that moment there was a car leaving the A34 and joining the M4 which was not being driven with its usual care and attention and whose two occupants - both nearer 60 than 50 - were behaving like demented sub-teens.

So it was in the hope of re-capturing a little of that euphoria that we were this day making the same journey in reverse, with Colin one of five due to go to post at Fontwell in the two miles six furlongs Manny Bernstein *Don't be Disqualified Again Showcase Steeplechase* (and no, I don't understand the origins of that title either).

Another aspect of Colin's character is the kind of track which suits. Unlike some horses, he doesn't care whether the course is left or right-handed and please don't tell the handicapper, but he doesn't seem to care over much about the weight he carries.

But on galloping tracks, the speedier horses get into their rhythm and Colin gets passed, other horses' backsides come into view and as already discussed, Colin goes into a sulk and doesn't want to play. So the trick is to find him flat tracks (undulations aren't his thing either) where the horses are twisting and turning and his jumping comes into play (always provided of course that it is one of his 'going' days). In the jargon, he wants tracks which favour the 'handy horse'.

In his excellent book, *The Course Inspector, The Times* racing correspondent, Alan Lee, says that Americans would not understand Fontwell. Nor, he adds, would racegoers in most other parts of the world, reared as they are on 'stereotyped, sliderule-flat, left-handed tracks.' The Fontwell hurdle track is just a mile round and 'inside it, a figure-of-eight chase course with dizzying cambers and corners.'

It is in fact the only figure of eight jumping course left (Windsor, sadly lost to jumpers, was the other one). Horses are constantly twisting and turning and it is its dizzying effect which gives us our chance. And Colin is not the only creature who finds it more difficult to keep track of circuits completed here than he does elsewhere. Stories are legion of jockeys riding a brilliant finish at Fontwell only to discover that they've put the effort in one circuit too soon.

In fact Colin brings a pretty good record here. His four career starts at the Sussex track have so far produced three wins and a second (two wins and a second under our ownership).

Mark you, he still has some way to go to match a horse called Certain Justice. *The Channel Four Racing Complete A-Z of Horse Racing* (another book for every serious racegoer's shelf) tells us that he won 14 races at the track, the last in 1965.

Any horse capable of dealing with the constant twists and turns of Fontwell on that scale certainly wouldn't have needed to be buried. Ask nicely and he would corkscrew down to the earth's core before you could say 'starter's orders'.

There are two other people who are fundamental to Colin's story, his trainer and his regular jockey. Dr. Philip Pritchard is the trainer and the only man who is both a Jockey Club - licensed trainer and NHS general practitioner as well as amateur jockey, racecourse doctor, house and horsebox - builder etc. etc.

Suffice to say that the Doc (as he's universally known) has been patient with both horse and owner. I do know that the Doc showed great promise as a trainee psychiatrist and he has needed it for both horse and human in this case, on the one hand working out the horse's foibles while on the other, dealing with the owner's reaction to them.

He is not with us today for the simple reason that he has taken Blazing Batman to Market Rasen where he gets third place (and spends half an hour wrangling with the stewards convinced he should have had second).

In his place to Fontwell comes Mrs Pritchard, a seeming slip of a girl, but in fact mother of two young sons, a chiropractor (for both horses and humans) who is in her early forties. She seems to have not done too well in this particular family raffle. Philip is taking one horse to Market Rasen (although in fairness he is the regular rider) whereas Teresa has got five horses (in two separate boxes) due to run at Fontwell - including saddling up three in one race.

Which brings us to jockeys. Colin's regular rider is Andrew Thornton, winner of the Gold Cup on Cool Dawn and a terrific second on Sir Rembrandt in 2004. After his last win for us at Fontwell, Andrew was in third place behind Messrs McCoy and Johnson in the jockeys table.★★ Andrew shuns the steam room favoured by many riders trying to make a weight and instead favours exercise to sweat it off. It is not unknown to see him jogging round racecourses (before racing I should add).

I have to confess this whole business of weight in racing makes me rather uncomfortable. Stripped, first thing in the morning and on a good day, I turn the scales at about $15^{1/2}$ stones. I am just over five foot eight inches tall. I am afraid a life in which the pleasures of the table have figured large have left their mark.

Picture the discomfort at Newton Abbot in July when, despite my message not to worry, a white-faced Andrew had stood in the parade ring and announced proudly that he had managed to 'do' the ten stones four pounds Colin was due to carry that day. His minimum is normally ten six or seven and I had said I would happily accept the extra few pounds overweight in return for his experience.

★★Despite a long lay off because of injury after the turn of the year, Andrew finished the season in fifth place with his best ever tally of 86 wins from 528 rides. Among them was his win at Ascot in November on Kingscliff - when the bit broke - which was voted by readers of the *Racing Post* the Ride of the Season.

I confess to a distinct feeling of unease, considering this chap is somewhat taller than me. The 40 inch waistband on my trousers was eased guiltily as was the 17 inch shirt collar at the sight of a professional who clearly hadn't had anything remotely serious to eat for several days.

One of the reasons Andrew originally got the ride is because he is much taller than the average at 5 feet eleven inches and because he also chooses to ride longer (just have a look at the length of his leg irons compared to many). His old-fashioned length of leg causes smiles among some but for us it means he can really shove and push, keeping nudging to give the horse the 'shove' part of the equation which is usually essential to get any sort of performance from Colin. The 'push' part comes from the arms and shoulders which will be doing just that for pretty much the whole race.

Very often when you see a jockey pushing and shoving on a horse when the race has just started, you can tear up your betting slips immediately. With Colin he is just being his natural self – craftiness, fettle and all.

The end result is surely one of the more bizarre sights in any winners' enclosure. Andrew, one of the fittest jockeys around, can often barely speak such has been the non-stop exertion when he gets off after a race. The horse, however, shows no sign of having even trotted, let alone competed in a three miles steeplechase. In a reverse of the standard situation, we have the rider legless, gasping for breath and looking in need of an oxygen tent – while the horse looks as if he has done no more than get up from his sun lounger.

The standing joke between us is that Andrew maintains he should be paid double for the effort involved in riding 'that monkey'. We counterpoint by saying that far from paying him double we are thinking of charging him the equivalent gym fees for the keep fit exercise it involves.

So Andrew Thornton is highly experienced, knows the horse inside out, is articulate and shrewd – and is unavailable to us today. He has been claimed by Jimmy Mullins, one of his regular trainers, and while we wish it wasn't so, it is entirely understandable. Jockeys are professionals and they must go with the people who provide their bread and butter.

Sometimes you get lucky. Robert Alner, his main trainer, very reasonably allowed Andrew to choose which horse to ride when he had a runner and when Klondike had won the first of his recent Fontwell races. Andrew picked right – and I quite rightly paid a public thank you to Mr. Alner after the race when I was interviewed in the winners' enclosure. But Colin is just one horse - the Alner and Mullins stables provide Andrew with umpteen rides in a season.

The news had been broken to me by Andrew's agent, Dave Roberts, a few days before the race. I have to say that when I first dealt with Mr Roberts I went a little warily. His reputation was as a man who doesn't suffer fools gladly. In fact I have found him helpful, reliable and absolutely straightforward. He may not have time for small talk but when you look at the list of clients he handles you can see why.

How he keeps happy a group of guys who are all fiercely competitive – despite the camaraderie of the weighing room - is a mystery. To handle both Mr McCoy and Mr Johnson at the same time, let alone all the others, must require skills certainly beyond my comprehension. Perhaps if he added Mr Arafat and Mr Sharon or Mr Trimble and Mr Adams to his long client list we might start to see some progress in the world.

I don't think it's too often that smaller owners like us get involved in quite this way - but with a doctor for a trainer it sometimes happens that the Doc is otherwise occupied.

In his place, and after a chat with the Doc, I opted for Tom Doyle, a jockey who had ridden another of our horses the previous season. So it was his name that appeared against the horse's name in the *Racing Post* which made us the

Spotlight selection and which had this to say about our chances: '... Klondike Charger back on his happy hunting ground can add to his record on the course.'

There was however one secret unknown to the *Racing Post* when they made their choice. It has remained a secret until now. This stupid owner - no blame attaches to Mrs Byrne - had had a serious senior moment.

Tom Doyle had indeed given our horse a decent ride in the race - the problem was I had really admired the effort put in by Noel Fehily on a Charlie Mann-trained 'monkey' called Villair. Mr Fehily's efforts in pushing and shoving for pretty well the whole race had resulted in his horse taking the No 1 spot when half a mile from home we looked all over the winners. This chap could be one for Colin, thought I, if A. Thornton should ever not be available.

When Tom Doyle appeared in the parade ring in our colours I realised my mistake. Please be a little understanding. After all I could hardly turn round at that point and say 'sorry we've got the wrong jockey.' So I said nothing - and until now the secret has stayed with me and my conscience.

As requested, Tom did his best to push and shove but was rather caught at the beginning when the others went off at a fair old lick while Colin was still in his sleep walking routine. The result - other horses' backsides and Colin not wanting to play. After less than a mile we knew it was not going to be our day (and Tom had already warned us that watering had produced ground which in the jockeys' opinion was 'dead' rather than the official 'good to firm').

As others started to tire, Colin redeemed something of the day by staying on for the last half mile or so and ran on in to third place, 25 lengths behind the winner - but three up on the fourth. That meant that as owners we took home £662 (the published prize money less twenty per cent for jockey and trainer). To this was added £250 for Sunday appearance money (to encourage owners to support Sunday racing) making a bit over £900. So even allowing for entry and jockey fees plus transport we were ahead on the day.

If only I could report such cheery news as a result of my dealing with the bookmakers at Fontwell. I had thought 3/1 a good 'early bird' price and laid £300 in the course Tote Credit Club.

I then laid another £100 to win at 7/2 (his SP was 100/30) in the ring. So that means with Jessie's fourth at Chepstow, my Tote credit account is where it normally is, pretty well at its limit. But in fairness I had won around £1,500 with Colin's two wins plus a bit for Jessie's third at 50/1. What else is the process of betting all about other than handing back all winnings to the bookies with, of course, a bit more for their trouble?

Chapter
4

Andy Stewart – Dream On

Andy Stewart came into my life in the parade ring at Fontwell. He had a horse called Phar From a Fiddle running in the same race as Klondike Charger. Normally the little huddles of connections in the parade ring eye each other more than a little furtively, each trying to work out which group are with each horse. And sometimes there can even be just a hint of something stronger. Colours and all, this is probably the nearest we get these days to the mediaeval joust.

None of that for Andy Stewart. He strode across with a sort of easy lope which reminded me of the politician-diarist Alan Clark. From the arm of a well-cut brown suit a hand came out and with total confidence, considerable charm and just the hint of a Clark-like drawl he said : 'Can I just say how much I enjoyed your book'(he was referring to my first effort *You Just Never Know*). Naturally I was flattered and we talked for a few moments, he explaining that he has a standing order with Waterstone's to have racing books sent to him as soon as they're published.

Later, after his horse had won, he was heading through the members' dining room for a post-race video viewing of his victory when he spotted self and wife. Would we care to join him in reviewing the race with a glass of champagne? Of course we did and with Joe Tizzard, his jockey that day, we enjoyed a glass or two and a chat. So that's how, some months later, I came to be sitting with him in a restaurant, one of two which he part owns in the capital, in the heart of the city of London.

Judy Stewart and jockey Ruby Walsh to the left and trainer Paul Nicholls and Andy Stewart to the right. In the middle, Cenkos, after another fine Cheltenham performance (Photo © Bernard Parkin & Cheltenham Racecourse).

The first thing to be said about A. Stewart is that he does not appear on any list as an owner. But his wife, Mrs J. Stewart does, and it is in her name that they currently have eleven horses with Paul Nicholls - including Cenkos, Le Duc, Le Roi Miguel - and two with Richard Phillips.

For several seasons Mrs Stewart has been the leading woman National Hunt owner, a position it clearly amuses her husband to make sure she maintains. But there is never any doubt in talking to him that he is the main driving force behind the enterprise. 'She's keen and knowledgeable and loves the big days at the top tracks - but she's not quite so keen on trailing to, say, Ludlow, on a wet November afternoon.'

'Besides', he says, in a line not being used for the first time, 'if she ever complains about the time I spend racing I simply say 'But darling, I'm just looking after your horses.'

There is also the male-female perspective in all this. 'When we've won a big race and we're in the winners' enclosure, my mobile will go off. It could be a friend saying well done or a journalist wanting to know about future plans. But hers will go off and it's a girl friend asking 'Where did you get that hat?"

Stewart has had quite a career in the city. He started as a 17-year-old clerk having been expelled from his minor public school 'for about 17 offences, one of which involved the cook's daughter.' He comes from a good solid middle class background. Both parents were doctors, but he was quite clear that after a lifetime of the *British Medical Journal* and the *Lancet* spreading, he says, 'gore over the Sunday lunch', medicine was not for him.

He has since helped create two sizeable City firms, selling the first and floating the second and in the process making two fortunes. He is now the president of Collins Stewart, the publicly quoted brokers, capitalised at around £1 billion with 2,500 employees spread around the globe. His duties as president don't sound overly onerous and I suspect that the City has not yet seen the last of Andy Stewart.

In the meanwhile he has the horses. When it comes to them Stewart is clear on a number of issues, not least the fact that he is not interested in buying other people's success. 'I wouldn't want to buy Best Mate, for instance, even if he was for sale.' That said, the three or four-year-olds he buys each year from France or Ireland – advised in both countries by a small team of what he considers the best judges – cost a six figure sum each. He would expect to sell or give away around four horses every year, replacing them with new ones. And no, he says emphatically, he would not wish to own more than he has. 'That's enough.'

Last year win and prize money totalled around £350,000. Does that seemingly very large amount cover all his costs? Well actually no. He reckons to cover the training fees but not the capital cost of the horses. 'If you were to treat them just as a business and put in a prudent depreciation charge - considering you pay a lot of money for a three-year-old which by the time it is a 12-year-old gelding it's worthless - you don't make any money.'

This then is serious money spent by a man and his wife on something which certainly at our lunch animates him more than the millions he has obviously made in the City. 'Does anybody make any money when they go to the opera? I enjoy doing what I do and everything I do in my life I enjoy doing to a high standard.'

Of horses in general he says 'They're honest. They don't lie, they're genuine and they rely on you. Sometimes they do let you down but not as much as people do. I get very attached to them.' And it's not just the horses. He has a glowing regard for some of the humans involved too.

He has Paul Nicholls as his main trainer 'because of, number one, the infrastructure he has created; and number two, because he concentrates on jumping horses and he is very dedicated.'

> He doesn't play golf, he doesn't go on holidays and as a result, as a young man, he has been able to train winners of the Gold Cup, the Arkle and the Champion Chase - and all in the same year. He's put together a complete package of facilities and staff. They're young, enthusiastic people, especially his assistant Jeremy Young - the whole comes as a fantastic package. Why do people go out and buy a Mercedes and not a Peugeot? Paul is the Mercedes Benz of training – not the Rolls Royce.

Then there's Paul Barber, Paul Nicholls' landlord, Somerset dairy farmer on a grand scale and co-owner of See More Business. Just days before we met, Mr Barber had sold Valley Henry out of the Nicholls yard to Graham Wylie, the Northern businessman who with Howard Johnston is making such an impact on jump racing. According to what looked like well-sourced press reports, the gelding had fetched at least £300,000.

Stewart says he doesn't know the actual amount that's

been paid but it looks like a price that couldn't be refused. And remember, he says, it will ultimately be good for racing. 'Paul Barber won't be spending any of that money on yachts or speedboats or whatever - all the proceeds will stay in racing.'

So Barber is obviously a shrewd deal-maker- but it's not that attribute which most impresses Stewart. 'He has a natural talent, an ability to look at a horse and know how he will develop. He looked at Le Roi Miguel when he first went to Paul Nicholls'yard. There he was, this thin, gangly animal but Paul Barber had the gift to look at this horse and say he would definitely train on and sure enough he won two Group Ones as a five-year-old. He's remarkable - and people like Tom Costello and Demi O'Byrne can do the same. They really are geniuses.'

Stewart's own horse odyssey began as a 15-year-old watching on black-and-white TV as Arkle won the Henessey, giving a stone to Mill House. 'It changed my perception of horses. From then I dreamed that I would be able to get involved and one day own a horse.'

Although he never rode much above hack standard he was always into jump racing, National Hunt and point-to-point. He remembers hitch-hiking up to see the Grand National in 1967 and the Cheltenham Festival was a must every year. And always that dream.

Of course, there were various 'incidents' along the way, like the time - still in his teens - when his mother, normally a couple of shillings each way punter, asked him to put for her the huge bet of £10 each way on Blakeney in the 1969 Derby. The family had a holiday home on the Norfolk coast near that very village. 'Not a hope' thought the young Stewart as he headed for the bookies with his mother's money. He decided to invest on another animal that was surely bound to win. When Blakeney came in at 10/1 he had a problem. And one which his father insisted was sorted at no loss to mother as a lesson to the son.

£125 was a lot of money back then, particularly for a young man earning not a lot but 'a couple of successful reverse forecasts at Catford dogs got me out of that one.' In fact, long before he owned even a piece of a horse, the smaller four-legged friends took centre stage. He found himself as the lynchpin of a greyhound partnership of five people with eventually 40 dogs, a couple of them running in some of the top greyhound races. 'The problem was it was all in my name and when some of the others turned round and said they only wanted to be involved with two of them, what was I supposed to do about the other 38?'

That's one of the reason he says that, apart from his wife, he avoids partnerships these days. But it wasn't so when he owned his half of a horse with a business colleague. 'I had a young family, a mortgage to worry about – all the normal things and I said I would have a share in Night Session provided I could watch him run in races on the TV on a Saturday afternoon. He was trained by Oliver Sherwood and he won seven on the trot.'

Then came Cenkos, his first wholly owned runner – and a horse who clearly has major claims on the Stewart affections.★★ He was originally with Kim Bailey, then went to Oliver Sherwood and is now at Paul Nicholls.

Stewart paid over six figures for him but he has already won over half a million pounds in prize money, taking in the Tingle Creek and the Queen Mother Celebration Chase as well as adventures in places as far-flung as Japan.

And yes, it was on the flight back from that country where Cenkos had run fifth of 15 in a race worth over £400,000 that jockey Timmy Murphy had the previously mentioned 'difficulties' which led to a prison term. It was Stewart, too, who lent Murphy the money for the treatment which has so successfully helped him get back into the saddle, including on Cenkos. They had a simple

★★Cenkos rounded off the Stewart season in fine style. He won the £58,000 Queen Elizabeth the Queen Mother Celebration Chase at Sandown on the last weekend of the 2003/2004 season.

arrangement. The jockey would re-pay the owner from his share of future winning rides.

Cenkos also takes centre stage in another Stewart gambling story.

Stewart likes to bet, but no longer on the scale he once did. His bets these days run into thousands, but not ten of thousands - something though that 'will make a significant difference.' A little while before the 2002 Queen Mother Champion Chase he'd had a word with Mike Dillon of Ladbrokes 'the most gentlemanly man in bookmaking.' What price, he enquired, would the bookie give him against Cenkos in that famous race?

The answer was 66/1. The owner took the price each way 'and on race day I was standing not far from the bookie at Cheltenham as the horses got to the top of the hill. There was my 66/1 shot going very nicely. I still think that if the going had been just a little faster we would have beaten Flagship Uberalles and Native Upmanship. Still it was nice to see a bookmaker doing a bit of worrying.' And not too bad a return either, I observed, on a horse which came third at those odds.

But it's definitely not the gambling that is the motivation- 'It doesn't really matter.' From some people that wouldn't quite ring true - but this is a man for whom money has to be seen in a different perspective. There are three homes, one in Sussex, one in Barbados and another in London - although it transpires that the London one is really two, one for Mr. and Mrs Stewart and next door for 'kids and visitors.'

He is also understandably proud of the fact that every pound he has and spends is money he has earned. But no life is entirely an idyll. This is a son who, when still young, had to cope when one parent committed suicide and the other died naturally not long afterwards. Even now, the sadness as he tells their story is obvious.

For whatever reason, he is these days a tireless fund raiser, actively involved in three charities, including a major racing one. The day after I met him he was due to take part in a two-mile sponsored fun run and as in so much he does, it was pretty obvious that A. Stewart intended to win (which he duly did).

Clearly it's the thrill of having horses run in and win big races that it's really about. The stories come tumbling out. 'The first big win - when Cenkos won the Arkle trial at Warwick … the time Le Duc★★ won at Liverpool at 33/1 but only after surviving the agony of a fifteen minute stewards enquiry … and last spring, when Le Roi Miguel, just five-years-old in awful conditions and without a pacemaker won the Silverstone Cup at Punchestown.' And 'he did it in such style, beating quality horses and you know he could have gone round again. It was the most exciting thing. I'm still coming down from that.'

Can he rationalise his passion for steeplechasing? 'Of course it can't be explained. But one thing does puzzle me. How excited we National Hunt owners get when our horses do well – the hats really are in the air - and how unexcited Flat owners are, with the exception of the Magniers. And it isn't just the big races. I still get a great thrill (with apologies to the owner) when Phar from a Fiddle beats Klondike Charger at Fontwell. That was great. My horse had been off for a year, he's got dodgy legs and it was great to see him back. I passionately love my horses and I really do care about them.'

There is a compressed energy about Stewart which is clearly the centre-spring of his success in life. He is on National Hunt racing's inside track, he knows everyone and is blessed with an extraordinary memory for horses and events. Those attributes have clearly served him well in both business and racing - but there was one occasion years ago when the famous memory let him down.

★★The five-year-old Le Duc was far from disgraced in the 2004 Arkle, finishing third of the 16 runners.

He had gone on a cheap charter holiday to Rhodes. The return flight was delayed and drink had been taken when he bet a pal ten shillings that he could get a date with one of the air hostesses. He couldn't remember too much, except he knew one had said yes and he found an address for a flat in his jacket with a date and time.

He turned up on the day at the appointed place and his heart sank when he found himself in a room with three girls, two of whom were 'not so good' and one who was. A two to one shot. Fortunately it was the good looking one who stood up when he looked vaguely round and said 'hello Julie.' This was in fact Judy, wife of 30 years, mother of their two sons, and the Mrs J. Stewart whose name appears in race cards.

Stewart's life is certainly not the average. Helicopters and planes to get to and from big races are the norm. And he cheerfully admits that he and his wife have never actually cooked a meal in their London home in the 14 years they've lived there.

Food and wine are his other great passion. If ever asked to appear on *Mastermind* he says that horses would not be his specialist subject. It would be the liquid stuff on which he would concentrate in the black chair.

But back with racing, Stewart has crystal clear views about the future of the sport. Not surprisingly for a man who has operated so successfully in the free market economy, he thinks there is only one sensible route.

Market forces will out. People in racing have to appreciate that bookmakers are owned by their shareholders. The directors have a duty to those shareholders and they aren't doing anything wrong under the rules.

I believe in the free market and I think people should be able to stage meetings whenever and wherever they like. This would transform the sport, opening up channels of new money.

But what, I asked, about the impact on fixture lists, breeding and smaller tracks?

'Some people are too pessimistic. These matters would be sorted out by the market for sound commercial reasons.' On one issue Stewart turns positively glacial. 'You do have to have doubts about the make-up and the age of the members of the Jockey Club. What would you make of a commercial company if quite so many members of the board went to one school, namely Eton. Would you invest?'

On some matters, Stewart is like just about every National Hunt owner. One pet hate is trainers who don't keep in touch. Not much chance of that it sounds with Paul Nicholls. They speak as many as three times a day in the run-up to a big race. Once a day otherwise.

Then there's excuses. 'Excuses from stockbrokers as to why a share has gone down can only be outdone by trainers as to why a horse hasn't won. I've made lots of mistakes – it really is best to admit them.'

Obsession with the weather as a race approaches is another one. 'It is ludicrous the way grown men can take whether or not it is drizzling quite so seriously.'

Then there's how he feels before a race. 'I get nervous, very nervous. But then it's great fun to be really nervous. On the other hand, the most infuriating thing is when people take racing too seriously. It is only fun.'

His ambition is common enough too, particularly in a man who has a positive disdain for flat racing and says he has no real interest in hurdling. 'Everybody's dream if they are in National Hunt racing is to win the Gold Cup. I'm on the look out for a decent three miler.'

But isn't it enough to have three or four horses for any one of which many people would happily hand over their right arm? 'Ah, but there's also quite a few for which nobody would even give their left toe-nail clipping.'

One definitely not in that category is Leroy's Sister, a four-year-old half sister to Le Roi Miguel and potentially something 'very special. She's had some injuries and we can't quite get her blood right – I'm very keen on blood tests. But she's done some very impressive work.'

Possibly the best yet? 'You can only dream.'

Chapter 5

David's Diary 2

OCTOBER 18

I spent the majority of my working life involved in making various kinds of radio and television programmes. In comparing the imagined programmes with the one actually transmitted *It Seemed a Good Idea at the Time* became my all - purpose programme title. In fact, come to think of it, it wouldn't make a bad inscription on my tombstone (although Mrs Byrne might have some interesting variants).

No matter - *It Seemed a Good Idea at the Time* certainly applied to our visit to Stratford. Klondike Charger was one of six due to run in a Class C steeplechase over just short of two and three quarter miles with total prize money (spread from first to fourth) of nearly £12,500.

I had been buoyed by half an hour on my calculator after the most recent contribution to funds from Fontwell. The tot-up told me that on the plus side, Colin's current total prize money for this season so far stood at £9,936. To that could be added the £7,000 he had won for his four seconds last season, making a total of £16,936 since we bought him.

On the other side of the column I calculated a total of £7,182 training fees (paid until the end of November this year); winter keep of £875; farrier bills of £400; transport costs of £1,900; and race entry costs of £570. To that we must add Colin's £6,000 purchase price. This makes a total of £16, 927.

So the figures show we have a horse that not only has paid for himself - but on which we are currently showing a profit of £9. Now I know that may not seem much but for a racehorse owner this is in fact a minor miracle (in fact forget the minor). We have had our thrills and fun for free. You can hope for no more. ★★

Just one thing though. Could nobody - and I mean nobody - tell Colin. He will never leave his stable again.

As well as the money matters, we also have a horse who - with all his little ways- has done us proud. To have a modest steeplechaser win two in a season is doing pretty well. Depending on how he goes, we will send him out two or three more times and then put him away for the winter.

Enter David's Good Idea. Everyone agrees that Colin is the kind of horse who if one day he got up before a race and everything was spot on in terms of track, going and weather might just say to himself, stretching in front of the shaving mirror: 'I know, I'll show them and give it a bit of a go today.' And if that happened to be before a half-decent race, who knows what might happen.

Now it so happens that the ground and the weather forecast were in our favour. Stratford has the reputation as a summer jumping track which delivers what it says. 'Good to firm and watering to maintain' was the official word. What's more there is a strip round the outside the watering does not seem to reach, opening up possibilities for horses like Colin, who want it on the firm side, provided they keep to the unwatered strip, even when it is officially good.

There were twelve horses entered at the five-day stage - and that number was halved before the off largely, I suspect, because the drought-like conditions had made owners and trainers reluctant to risk good horses - several of whom would have been making their seasonal debuts - on ground that was going to be too firm for many.

★★The later and, it has to be said, more detailed analysis of costs in Chapter Seven, told a somewhat different story. But this is what I believed at the time. And anyway, events in May changed the picture again.

Normally any sensible owner will be guided by his trainer about which race the horse runs in but when I explained my thinking to the Doc, he agreed it was worth a crack. The problems included the weight the horse would carry and the quality of the opposition.

This was a race open to horses handicapped up to 135. Top weight is 11stones 12 pounds and bottom weight is 10 stones. Our horse is currently off a handicap mark of 95. That 40 pounds difference means that we should be carrying nine stones against the top-rated horse. The minimum weight is 10 stones – so that means we are, in racing jargon, a stone out of the handicap.

So it was in the frame of mind that 'we know we aren't going to win, but let's have a nice day out and see what happens' that we set out with two friends – both in their early sixties and both never having been to a race meeting before. Mrs Byrne, it should be said, had benefited from my 121st explanation of handicap ratings and 'being out of the handicap' but was still none the wiser.

Lunch, never a small matter in my life, took the form of a picnic in the car park there being no room in either the Stratford members' restaurant or the excellent seafood operation.

God – or whoever is the sponsor of Good Ideas – had smiled upon us. We ate smoked salmon sandwiches and drank champagne as the sun shone down and, in between mouthfuls and gulps, I tried to explain the intricacies of the racecard to our two racing 'virgins'. I decided, however, to keep away from explanations about 'being out of the handicap'. Fortunately, with so much to take in, they didn't ask what the racecard summary about Colin meant. 'Stiff task from out of the handicap' it said. Strangely enough, neither did Mrs Byrne.

The jockey situation had been more of a muddle than usual. Andrew Thornton would have added more weight (and so have increased the amount we were out of the handicap). I would have accepted the overweight for his experience – but when Dave Roberts rang me it looked anyway as if Andrew had been claimed by a regular trainer for a reopened race at Kelso. Dave offered me several of his jockeys who could do ten stones.

Now the Doc is not only a trainer, he is also a highly experienced rider who knows the jockeys as a rival. He also has treated most of them as a racecourse doctor. I decided it was time to let all that experience take over.

We could have put up a conditional. These are the apprentices who have claims of seven, five or three pounds, their claim dropping as they win races, until the day comes when they have to take their chances without the weight incentive designed to encourage trainers to give them opportunities. Their allowance takes weight off the horse's back – and in our case could have reduced the amount Colin was 'out of the handicap' by up to half a stone.

Against that we have a tricky character who is nobody's idea of an easy ride. The Doc also says that he has far more problems getting conditionals to ride to orders than he does their more experienced colleagues.

So it is we have Roddy Greene in the saddle. He can do the ten stones, will ride to orders and is strong enough to shove and push says the Doc. Roddy regularly rides for Martin Pipe – although I am sure A.P. McCoy will one day persuade the champion trainer he should ride all his horses, even when there are four in the same race.

We take our 'virgins' into the saddling enclosure to discover that Colin is at his most laid back. His major effort seems to be going – not entirely successfully – into keeping his eyes open. The man who had the Good Idea begins to wonder.

Into the parade ring we go and Colin starts to take some interest in the proceedings, at one point even passing another horse. But like Colin, we are quite a relaxed group when Roddy appears in our silks. He has been well briefed already by the Doc and Andrew Thornton (all part of the weighing room intelligence network which has got more than a little to do with self-preservation).

With me giving one more reminder not to get left at the start, he's up in the saddle with my usual 'Good luck and come back safe.' The next horse behind him is in fact ridden by Andrew who gives us a cheery wave and gets one back in return (afterwards, in the owners' and trainers' bar, he confirms that he was expecting to go to Kelso - and how delighted he is to have 42 winners in the bag, keeping him in third spot in the jockeys' championship).

We watch the race from the viewing area which is just off the new owners' and trainers' bar (like so many trainers, the Doc prefers to watch the TV coverage). Just before the start it's obvious Roddy has got the message about not being left. As they circle, he's like the kid at the party determined not to be left with the parcel when the music stops.

Credit to him, when the tapes go up he's off in front and even before the first fence the course commentator notes how he is already pushing and shoving - and how wide he is running on the track, determined to go on that strip which has not been artificially watered.

There are 16 fences to be jumped in the race and Colin is in the lead until the 9th. Of course he has covered considerably more ground than the others because the jockey has done as asked and kept the horse on the firmest ground on the outside. But class will out. Colin always has to be shoved and pushed but nonetheless on a going day against his peer group he jumps well and travels o.k. Today it is obvious the others are travelling far more comfortably as we go into the final circuit. Over a distance which is his minimum and against better quality horses, by the 12th fence he is weakening and they all go past.

Roddy gives him a couple of cracks of the whip to see if there is anything left and when it is obvious there's not, he desists. We are beaten a distance, with A.P. McCoy just getting the Toby Balding-trained favourite, Duchamp, home against the top handicapper, Carbury Cross, making his seasonal reappearance.

If there is truth in that old saying about 'Putting Your Money Where Your Mouth Is' at least the originator of the Good Idea had not suffered too badly. I had invested a total of £35 each way in our chap so at least the monetary wounds were not too deep.

In fact after the race I bumped into one of racing's characters in the shape of Henry Ponsonby. Henry (a man as like his name as you are ever going to meet) was one of the originators of the racing syndicate in Britain.

It was in one of his syndicates that we had our first taste of winning. He told me the horse that did the winning, Secretary of State, now a 15-year-old, was living out a happy and healthy retirement down on the Devon coast.

We talked about this and that – including Henry's appearance in the public prints as an 'advisor' to Sir Alex Ferguson, who has syndicate shares in two of Henry's horses.

It is of course Sir Alex who is involved in the spat over the stud career of the prolific group winner on the flat, Rock of Gibraltar, whose value as a stallion runs into many millions. Matters are not made any less interesting by the fact that John Magnier – the man with whom Sir Alex is in disputation – is, along with legendary Irish gambler, J.P.MacManus, the owner of more than 20% of Manchester United.

Ho hum. Sounds as if the lawyers will have a field day as two men – neither of whom is famous for their sweetness and light – stand firm.

Henry told me he was paying his first visit to Stratford since 1985. He had come to see his four-year-old with good form on the flat in Germany make his debut in a maiden hurdle. Clearly Henry fancies the horse's chances and when he tells me its name I make sure the 'virgins' and Mrs Byrne are 'on'. Fleet Street (the centre of the journalistic trade in my day) is the horse and he obliges impressively at 3/1, putting right any losses incurred earlier and giving us, as the racecourse commentator said, a name for the notebook.

So it was we made our way home. It did seem a good idea at the time - and even owners have to be humoured sometimes.

OCTOBER 26

There we were, four of us, over-coated but outdoors, enjoying the late autumn sun, drinking champagne and eating sandwiches. All around, Somerset hills covered in trees in their autumn glory. What a summer it has been, particularly for us owners of firm ground horses. But all good things must come to an end and rain is forecast for the coming week. This could quench the parched earth as well as reduce the amount of hair-tearing about ground conditions which is now a commonplace throughout racing.

With four horses in training or about to go into training - and three of them needing some cut - I too would welcome it. And in truth my balding pate will only stand a very modest amount of hair-tearing.

Could this meeting at Wincanton, in whose owners' and trainers' car park we are standing, be the last serious chance this season for Klondike Charger to add to his magnificent overall £9 profit in our ownership?

I have always thought that the football team manager who, in his pre-match chat to his players, advised them to 'get their retaliation in first' had a point. Why wait until you know the result to drink champagne in celebration? You're still breathing aren't you?

In that spirit, self, Mrs Byrne and the judge and his wife raised our glasses to what might be. The judge, it should be said, was previously a very successful Q.C. and his wife is a senior university lecturer in law. So as the second bottle slipped down – and yes, Mrs Byrne drank water and drove home – I couldn't help thinking that if one had to be called before the stewards for any reason, today was the day. But only, of course, if one's learned friends could come too.

Now how had we come to choose Wincanton? Let me briefly explain for newcomers to the process. Every week a calendar of upcoming races is produced by Weatherbys, the family firm which has administered racing ever since Noah and his Ark found themselves marooned at a water jump. They work four weeks in advance for ordinary races but give notice in due time for the major events where different conditions apply.

In the calendar you will find the terms and conditions listed for all the combinations that the rules of racing permit and to which the race planners of the British Horseracing Board have agreed. In jump racing, they range from 'bumpers' of less than two miles to the four and a half miles of the Grand National. On the flat there's everything from five furlong sprints to two miles plus.

The key questions include: does my horse meet the age, sex and handicap rules? The age and sex rules are pretty straightforward. The horse either is or is not male or female and is either a three-year-old or a four-year-old. But the handicap mark is a different matter and offers an important option. As well as telling you the category of race (A to H), the conditions for handicap races will also say something like 0-115 or 0-130.

Each horse is of course re-assessed by the handicapper each time he or she runs so the handicap mark can move, like our other 'investments' (ho, ho, ho), both up and down. So if your horse is rated 139, well, lucky you but he will not be allowed to run in either of the above races. On the other hand if your horse is top-rated at 130 he will face the prospect of having to carry the maximum permitted weight of 11stones 12 pounds. For the person with a horse rated

110 in the same race, the 20 pounds difference will result in jockey and saddle totalling 10 stones 6 pounds.

If however the owner of the horse off 110 fancies a lower-rated race, say 0-115, he or she will have to accept that there is a real possibility the horse will carry $11\frac{1}{2}$ stones. So you have the classic dilemma - do I run against better quality horses off a low weight; or do I prefer he takes his chance carrying a big weight against lower-rated animals? It's for you and your trainer to decide.

For those of us who left full-time education at the age of 17 - not long after Noah set sail - clutching five O levels (two attempts), all this mathematics does not come easy. Particularly so as the score in my Maths O level was nought to 25 (for the sake of the nation I hope there are very few entries in that particular race). And incidentally no science subjects grace the yellowing list of passes. The grounds for that were the monks who ran the ghastly hell-hole I attended who looked at my mock O level science paper and announced 'considering I had been there five years, they were not going to have the school disgraced.' Mrs Byrne, my helpmeet in all matters, is not much use in this particular department. She hasn't even a 0-25 O level in either maths or science to offer.

Still, for one's sport one must work hard so the family abacus and fingers are in constant use. In fairness, how the younger generation cope with all these stones and pounds not to mention furlongs and guineas central to racing's calculations is another mystery. The thought that some bright spark might want to change it to all that newfangled stuff is enough to make this man demand an immediate large drink - as long, of course, as it's a pint.

Now, as well as the hard sums, you will also have to allow for the distance of the race and the kind of track - tight or galloping, left or right-handed - which you think will best suit your runner. Also, what are the ground conditions likely to be when you want to run and will they suit? You may also have a jockey who knows the horse well – will he be available to ride that day?

If you are happy on all those counts, does the race fit in your overall plan for the animal (always provided there is one) and as an owner, if you want to see your horse run, does your diary permit?

You can of course be a very happy owner, cheering home your horse without bothering about any of the technical stuff I have outlined. But on the other hand, there are plenty of us who find the other stuff fascinating without in any way diminishing the marvel of seeing our horse in our colours line up, all the technical stuff for the moment forgotten in the thrill of the race. Later, when you ponder on the race, you wonder did you get the technical stuff right or wrong and what have you learnt for next time.

Many trainers see it as their job to plot when and where the horse runs – but with the Doc, in whose stable Klondike Charger does his Rip Van Winkle impersonations, we have a trainer keen to encourage as much involvement as possible.

He will offer advice and suggestions but he has absolutely no objections to owners who want to do their own thing. Conscious that Colin would not get his preferred ground for ever and also that he stands up well to running frequently – as his two wins and a second in 12 days in August demonstrated – we had agreed on all the likely races for him throughout October.

After our Stratford run the real prospects came down to three – Wincanton on the Sunday; Cheltenham on the Tuesday; and Stratford (again) on the Thursday.

The rules state that you have to enter your horse by 12 noon five days before the race (six days in the case of Sunday racing). By the evening of entry day you will be able to see on the *Racing Post* website (or in the paper the next day) the other horses which may be taking part.

You will be able to work out what weight your horse

could carry - provided the top-weighted horse stays in. Remember the top-rated will carry 11 stones 12 pounds even if it is a 0-115 race and the top-rated horse is off a handicap mark of 100. The difference in that horse's rating and your own will decide the weight your chap might carry.

To help, 24 to 36 hours later the *Post* will update the race and instead of alphabetical order with overall ratings they will sort the possibles into handicap order, top weight first, and showing the weight each one will carry - provided everybody stays in (which is very unlikely). By 10 a.m. on the day before the race your trainer (although I have occasionally done it) will need to have told Weatherbys by phone or, increasingly, by computer, if your horse is staying in.

By around 11 a.m. the television text services (and about an hour later on the internet) will list the horses that are running with weight adjustments for the drop-outs. They will also give you indications of likely starting prices (but they are only indications) as well as most of the jockey bookings. The rest of those have to be settled by 1 p.m., Mr Roberts and his fellow agents telling trainers (and sometimes owners) who is available and who's not.

The timetable is strictly adhered to. The newspapers and the racecard printers have their work to do so that all is in place for the next day's racing. Extreme changes in going conditions or a late medical problem with a horse (which needs a vet's certificate) will allow you to withdraw- but 99 times out of a 100, once you are in you're in.

There is room for manoeuvre in the sense that you can weigh up your options in several races, always allowing for the fact that it will cost a relatively small amount (taken against the overall costs of training) to enter each race. £20 to £50 per race would be a rough guide.

So with the Doc we agree Wincanton was the most likely - but Cheltenham on the Tuesday was another option. We didn't have to say whether we would go to Wincanton until 10 a.m. on Friday morning. That meant that we could look at the Cheltenham horses on the Thursday afternoon.

It was not a difficult choice. There were only ten entered at Wincanton, 20 (including some quite serious horses) at Cheltenham. We were in the middle of the handicap at Wincanton (a 0–110)and just out of it at Cheltenham (a 0–125). But just to be on the safe side, Klondike Charger also went into the hat for Stratford on the Thursday.

So far so good – but then your man upstairs decided that it was time to shuffle the pack. With firm ground in prospect at Wincanton only four would go to post. Colin, off a handicap mark of 95, would be lugging top weight over 3 miles one and a half furlongs – and including 21 fences – in the Tote Exacta Handicap Chase, one of six races which made up the card for the course's annual charity day.

We had last been here exactly two years ago and the first thing to say is what a transformation has been achieved at Wincanton without losing the 'feel' of the place. Every racetrack has its own style and character. Some of us worry that we would be losing something very special if all the TV money which is flowing into the sport (and thank goodness for it) would be wasted if everything finishes up being the same. Just think about the 'transformation' of British high streets.

Wincanton stages some top flight races but the facilities were getting more than a little careworn. Not any more.

We had two runners when we last came, including one in the main event of the day, the class A Fieldspring Desert Orchid steeplechase with £35,000 prize money on offer. This time the race itself provided two delights. First, Desert Orchid himself was ridden past the stands just before the race.

He is still held in enormous affection by the jumping public. Hard to believe that as he came past, splendid chest to the fore, that he would be 25 in just a few months or that it is 12 years since he last competed. Applause and smiles all round, particularly when the old boy made it perfectly plain that he would be more than happy to take on the 'youngsters' lining up to run in HIS race.

Second, in the race itself, Edredon Bleu, a mere stripling of eleven, gave an exhibition of jumping that was simply splendid. Those of us who were there at Cheltenham for his heart-stopping Queen Mother Champion Chase win in 2000 will never forget it – but the way he set a new course record at Wincanton that day will stay in the memory too.

'Sheer class' said the judge (the criminal not the racing one) – and on that one, in his lexicon, he was 'bang to rights'.

On our way from viewing that race to prepare for the somewhat humbler fare on view in *our* race, who should walk in but Trainer Evans, who had a runner in the last. Time for a word about Jessie MacDougall, who had been found to have a minor back problem following her run at Chepstow.

What nobody knows is whether she did her back in the race or the next day when, bucking, kicking and squealing, she celebrated being let out into the field.

Either way she has been on light duties but the trainer says she is much improved and is to start cantering again the next day. With that news, we headed to the saddling enclosure where it wasn't long before Mrs Byrne and Mrs Pritchard (the Doc being 'on call' today) fell into a detailed discussion about just how sick they felt when a race was in progress. The trainer's representative confessed in the course of this cheery chat that it helped if the horse had no chance.

There was a point as he was saddled up at which I swear Colin was on the point of dropping off to sleep. The eye-lids drooped and he looked for all the world much like the rest of the male population on a Sunday afternoon. The parade ring itself produced some improvement, he being by-passed by only one horse keen to proceed at a speed greater than ours, the horse made snail.

The *Racing Post* said of his chances : 'Klondike Charger has as good a chance as any if back to his best … but his recent efforts have lacked sparkle.' That seemed pretty fair to me, although one has to admire any writer who can contrive a sentence which includes the words 'Klondike Charger' and 'sparkle'.

In gambling terms, I did think he had a serious chance – but I had decided to confine myself to a £200 on the nose on credit. A trip to the betting ring saw him very much on the drift, the outsider of four at 15/2. Oh woe is me - such value, thought I, and lumped on another £200.

Now Colin ran a decent enough race and was in the lead or thereabouts until four out .The weight was too much (he was giving a stone to the eventual winner) and he also jumped left at a couple of fences and then made a hash of the second last. Wincanton is never going to be an ideal course for him, the bends are too easy and it favours the galloper – but with a small field and firm ground it was definitely worth a try.

We had at least added to our winnings with a third prize of £613 plus £250 Sunday appearance money. With transport, jockey and entry fees taken off, we were still more than £500 ahead. Such a pity that my gambling bills are treated as a very different matter to the horses in the Byrne household accounts.

As usual in the winners' enclosure when Andrew Thornton got off his back, there was more blowing from the jockey than the horse. 'Race him again quick' said the gasping jockey, the horse looking for all the world as if he had had no more than a stroll in the autumn sunshine. When told that we had an entry for Stratford on Thursday, Andrew immediately panted 'go for it.' When told that the race was over three and half miles a look which had more than a touch of desperation came across his face.

There are times when racing's rules can be a trial, but not always. It was at that point Mr. Thornton had to leave us – to weigh in.

OCTOBER 30

So it was, partly at least because of Mr. Thornton's advice, that I found myself standing in the parade ring, benefiting from both driving wind and freezing rain, just before the start of the Class D (0-125) Carter Jonas Handicap Chase for five-year-olds and upwards over three and half miles.

I was by no means alone - but I was without A. Thornton, jockey, who had chosen to take his chances in two races at Towcester. As always, fair enough, but I couldn't help noting that neither of the races was over three and a half miles (although it has to be said, one of them was just over three miles and he did win it on a horse which had been off the track for 430 days).

Also absent was Mrs Byrne. She had headed to Leeds for her annual trip to her longest-standing friend. Nor was racing partner Terry there - he was off fishing in Ireland.

And neither was the Doc. He had intended to be there, planning in typical style to slot the race between his morning and evening surgeries in Gloucestershire. But then had come an emergency call from Towcester. Was there any chance he could step into the breach and pop on his racecourse doctor outfit?

Considering that without doctors in attendance race meetings cannot be staged, I made no complaint when he rang and explained as I was arriving at the track. Considering this was Klondike Charger's fourth visit to the races this month and indeed his third visit in 12 days, I could hardly play the greenhorn owner.

You may imagine that the phone call also told me that Mrs Pritchard was stepping into the breech. Well, yes and no. Today it was the turn not of the Doc's wife but the lady who was previously Mrs Pritchard - the Doc's Mum, Margot. It certainly wasn't a problem for me. Margot and I get on well and she it was who was in charge when Colin registered his first Fontwell win for us in August.

Just to complete today's family picture, the Doc's Dad was driving the lorry. The fact that the Doc's Dad now lives in Inverness and was divorced from the Doc's Mum more than 40 years previously was neither here nor there. Nobody can say that come what may this isn't a family business.

You may be thinking at this point that we were perhaps a little short of experienced hands for the tacking up. Not a bit of it. The Doc had called in some favours to help and told me that the jockey would also be on hand. But when the jockey picked up a spare ride in the race before ours, he too had called in some favours.

The end result - jockeys, travelling head lads, and stable staff galore, with barely enough room in the saddling box for the horse let alone the owner. I swear Best Mate doesn't have more top-rate help before the Gold Cup.

The jockey in question was James Davies, the conditional rider attached to Brendan Powell's stable. He was also the jockey who had ridden the horse which had beaten us at Wincanton on Sunday. With neither Andrew Thornton nor Roddy Greene available to us, I had opted for James from the list offered because he does bring a valuable five pound claim with him - but more importantly this is a chap with real talent, clearly destined for stardom.

His Sunday winner was the 20th so far this season and provided he can steer clear of injury, goodness know what it could be at season's end. He is also living proof that it pays to note the breeding in all aspects of racing. James is the son of Hywel Davies who won - among many races - the Grand National on Last Suspect.

James is also very young, looking no more than about eleven (in fact he's 19) to my admittedly ageing eyes, when complete with riding cap and colours. He also arrived in the parade ring not without advice about the wonders of riding Klondike Charger. It transpired that: a) the Doc had had a word; b) Andrew Thornton had found a quiet corner of the weighing room; and c) James's boss, Mr Powell, had had a chat about following instructions.

God bless them all – but Margot had also arrived with another set of written instructions which she had been told to read out loud to him. 'I decided it was best to just let him read them himself' she confided to me. And then the Doc had asked me to run through them one more time in the parade ring before the off just to make sure.

Just in case there's a jockey out there who's decided after all that's been said that Colin is their dream ride, let me pass on the standard instructions everyone who rides him other than Andrew Thornton (who devised most of them) gets to hear.

One: make sure he is up with the leaders when the tapes go up.

Two: don't use the whip on him other than to get a leading position at the first fence and not again before the second last fence.

Three: always look for the fastest ground (at Stratford that means running on the far outside where the track's watering equipment doesn't work so well).

Four: don't let him idle.

Five: don't give up.

Six: make sure he finishes.

So when the young – and, it has to be said, charming – Mr Davies appeared in the parade ring and came over to us I had decided that the one thing he didn't need was for me to go through it all again. 'You must be sick to death of people telling you how to ride this horse' is what I actually said – which at least got the conversation underway with a smile.

I always feel a bit for the younger jockeys when they walk into the parade ring. They are faced with eager owners, old enough to be their grandfathers, who they've never met before and who want to tell them a whole string of things about a horse which they have yet to see let alone sit on.

Colin should have been carrying 10 stones 1 pound, but thanks to James's claim that was down to nine stones ten, a valuable help in this marathon and quite a difference to the eleven stones twelve he had been under just four days before.

All that said, I can't say I really envied James as he was legged up. I suppose that in owning a horse you are by proxy getting something of the thrill of riding. Sometimes you feel you are riding such is the concentration as you measure each fence through the binoculars. And, of course, you don't have to be an owner to see what a thrill it must be to race ride.

On the other hand here's James, with everybody having told him what a lazy so and so he's just got aboard, and with three and a half miles ahead of him. What's more, I knew – but James didn't - that the rain which had started an hour before our race plus the cold wind which felt as if it had come straight from Siberia were not going to help our cause. I was sure Colin, as always, would have taken the shades, suntan cream and swimming trunks with him on to the lorry.

So it was with rather more fervour than usual I said the 'Good luck - and come back safe' mantra.

I should not have worried. James gave him a cracking ride and we were there or thereabouts until just before the last. As they turned for home he looked to have a serious shout. 'I really thought we were going to be in the shake-up' said the jockey, unsaddling in the third spot in the winners' enclosure.

He also said: 'Smashing horse. He jumped from fence to fence. I'd love the chance to ride him again.' I checked and yes, these words were coming from the jockey in our colours.

Daft I know, we'd come third in a four-horse race (in which the fourth horse had fallen) beaten 12 lengths by the winner and I'd lost another £50 – but I felt elated. I had wanted to try him over this distance, the furthest he had ever run. He was anything but disgraced.

The truth is we need to come down the handicap from our current 95 mark (he was off 87 when he had won the first of this summer's races) but today's winnings of £524 put us around £1,000 ahead, all costs included. And never mind that - we've had some splendid fun and infuriating though he is, he's given us a couple of days this summer we won't ever forget. Lucky us.

There was one other scrap of conversation in the winners' enclosure. As I praised James's riding and he praised the horse, I said that he wasn't as out of breath as Andrew when he gets off the horse. 'Well yes' said our rising star with all the untarnished honesty of the young 'but he's older than me.'

On the way home I speak to the Doc who's watched TV coverage of the race. We agree that Colin's run a cracking race but after eleven races that's enough. He can go on his holidays at my daughter's place, a job well done. The average steeplechaser runs only about four times in a season - we've been to the races with him eleven times and won twice. He's fit and sound and is still only nine.

It falls to the lucky few to own the stars of the jumping game (or any other). Colin is certainly not a star or anywhere near it - but if this is all about having fun, well we've certainly had that. And whatever else he might be, nobody could accuse him of being boring and predictable.

NOVEMBER 10

The same description could fairly be levelled at the Doc who had persuaded me it was a good idea to run Klondike Charger just once more at Fontwell today. And for a rather special reason.

What had happened was this: I had taken a call from the Doc with just five minutes to go to the deadline for five-day entries. He had been using his trainer's computer link to Weatherbys (unavailable to mere mortals) to monitor the number of entries for Fontwell. The trainers can see the number of horses who have declared - but not of course their names.

With the weather dictating that many tracks were continuing to have the word 'firm' somewhere in their official description, fields were remaining much smaller than normal. The Doc gets some of his fun (besides the training, the riding and the racecourse doctoring) from operating within the rules of racing but having a keen sense of, how shall we say, the outer boundaries. It is clearly the job of a trainer to find the easiest races for his charges - and the Doc takes that part of his job very seriously. Small fields mean less opposition and the opportunity to pick up place money.

'I know we had agreed to turn him away ...' said the Doc but then said he had spotted there were two suitable races at Fontwell, one with only three entrants and the other with four. I turned down the three miles and two option, the one with just three entrants, straightaway. Colin had done his stuff over the long distances - enough.

But I suspect it was the second one - over just two miles and two furlongs - that the Doc really wanted me to take up. Some years before, I had been in the Doc's yard when a blonde-haired seventeen-year-old by the name of Ollie had appeared.

Fresh out of jockey school, Oliver Dayman had the makings, but racing is a hard road to travel and he had not always found it easy knuckling down to the daily grind. I admired his spirit and the way he went about his business both at home and when he took horses to the races. The talent was obvious and encouraged by the Doc, he had applied for and got his amateur licence.

For several weeks in the summer he had starved himself ready for his first ride in public. And then the meeting was abandoned because of the ground. All Ollie's efforts had been for nought.

I had a quiet word with the Doc and said that if there was ever a suitable race, Colin could be the ideal carriage for a young rider making his debut. In his time the horse has clouted a good few fences but somehow that PhD in looking after yourself has meant – up until now (and all fingers and toes crossed) - he has never fallen in any of his 37 runs over hurdles and steeplechases. Somehow, he always manages to stick out a hoof to stay on an even keel. As my daughter who has ridden work on him (and teaches showjumpers) says: 'Dad, he really knows what he's doing. If you just sit tight, he sorts it out.'

Somebody has to give the young 'uns a go. So with Mrs Byrne's agreement, that's why Klondike Charger runs this day, which just happens to be Ollie's 19th birthday, in the Hardings Bar and Catering Services Amateur Riders' Handicap Chase (Class F) for horses rated 0-100. The distance is way short of his best - but today the taking part (and the coming back safe) really is more important than the winning.

At least the handicapper has shown willing. He has dropped Colin down 4 pounds for his recent experiences, so he is now off a mark of 91.

There are just five runners going to post. Once more the long arm of the Doc has taken a hand to make sure that Ollie and Colin face the minimum number of opponents possible. The rules state that if there are less than 10 entries at the five-day stage, the race can be reopened. The Doc wasn't having that.

Having got my agreement and just before the deadline, he entered another six horses besides Colin. Funnily enough those six didn't make it to the overnight stage.

Family commitments meant there was no way I could make it to see the race at the track. I decided I would break my journey in the Shropshire market town of Much Wenlock to watch the race.

Mrs Byrne - Lesley Bootiman professionally - did go and this is how she saw it.

I suppose it was inevitable even before I set off for Fontwell with horsey-daughter that the question of what to wear would come up. This is not as frivolous a topic as you might think. I'm not talking 'Ascot' here - rather practicalities and above all 'not letting the horse down'.

First, in my view clothes for racing have to be practical — I can't be bothered with teetering on stilettos while I negotiate the steps of the stand or, literally, run to the unsaddling enclosure to get the jockey's instant summing up of the race. 'Over the top' hats are also out — they annoy other racegoers because they hinder their view and anyway it's hard to use binoculars when a bunch of flowers and cherries are tickling your nose.

Other 'no-nos' are clothes without pockets (where do you put your binoculars/racecard/Racing Post?) and handbags that won't go over your shoulder. You need hands free to pat the horse, hold the horse, shake the jockey's hand (more of that in a minute) and mark your racecard.

On the other hand I don't want to turn up as a scruff. Race courses are unfortunately following the trend for 'dressing down' and I wish they wouldn't. Men in particular fall only too happily into the ripped denim and T-shirt look in summer and dreary anorak for winter, when only a couple of years ago it was assumed that going to races involved a tie, a decent jacket or overcoat and probably a smart trilby. It added to the sense of occasion and, let's be frank, men, particularly of a certain age and shape, look better for a little tailoring. It seems to me that racegoers - both men and women - at the northern tracks have a thing or two to teach their southern cousins in these matters.

If you're an owner there's another reason for being smart - the horse. I know it may sound odd but it is important that the horse is well represented. After all stable staff have spent hours 'turning him out' to look his best and when you stand in the centre of the parade ring it's good to look as if you care. And then there's the formal routine the jockeys follow when they arrive to mount your horse. They arrive, resplendent in your colours, they raise one hand to their caps and then they shake hands with the owners.

If you look as if you've rolled in from a mucky job on the farm I feel it's disrespectful to them and the challenge they're about to undertake.

So what do I wear? In the summer - a casual dress or lightweight suit, low heeled shoes and a Panama hat. In the winter it's a very different story. The cold winds of Chepstow taught me a long time ago that freezing at a racecourse takes away all the fun. So its layers for me, overcoat, boots, two pairs of socks (sometimes over tights!) and a trilby hat.

But as horsey daughter reminded me on the journey — its easy to 'do smart' or to 'do warm'; it's not easy to do both at the same time. I think we managed.

Horsey daughter was keen to come with me — she is close to Klondike as he was pre-trained by her and is going back to her yard immediately after the race for his 'winter holiday'. But she is also keen to see the young jockey-to-be make his debut. Having ridden out with him on many a freezing cold, wet morning and seen the day-to-day slog involved before a stable lad is allowed to ride in a race she wanted to cheer him on for his big day.

We meet up with the rest of the pair's supporters and the group has a heavily female bias. There's the trainer's wife (Teresa always manages to look smart despite running around to dance in attendance on jockeys, horses and owners); the trainer's mother Margot, (resplendent in smart overcoat with velvet collar); a girlfriend of the young jockey who's brought her mother (both managing the warm but smart trick). And most important of all, Oliver's very smart, and very nervous, mother along with (the only male) his father sporting a smart trilby. We're all obviously keen not to let down horse or rider.

I quickly realise just how nervous Oliver's parents are. He doesn't come from a 'horsey background' — they have no idea from where this obsession developed. They only know that as a young teenager he begged rides on horses and was interested in nothing but going to Jockey School. And in that way that sons have, he had tried not to worry them so not only have they never seen Oliver gallop a horse or jump a horse but they have never seen him take a horse up to trot or canter. There is a particular reason for Oliver's protective attitude. He is the youngest in a close family of six children. An elder brother died tragically of meningitis and much of the family's time is spent raising money for a meningitis charity.

The rest of the family is gathered to watch the race in betting offices around the country while Mum and Dad are bravely coping with their first ever proper visit to a racecourse.

I try to be reassuring - Klondike is very experienced; he's also very laid-back; he keeps out of trouble and he fiddles his fences so expertly he has so far never fallen in a race. They give me that look that says 'there's always a first time'.

We head off to the saddling enclosure where we find Oliver helping to saddle up the horse. This is not something a jockey would always be expected to do before a race and certainly the top jocks don't do it - but Oliver has a long way to travel to reach those dizzy heights. He knows Teresa could do with his help and also he's double checking that everything is fastened as he would wish it.

I discover from Margot that he had been on the horse at seven that morning, missing breakfast, so he could try out different stirrup lengths – I approve. He's leaving nothing to chance. I also suspect that he wanted a bit of quiet time with Klondike to establish a bond to carry them round safely. We're not privy of course to the private words between jockeys and horses - probably just as well! He's also spent every night in the gym (after a day of mucking out and schooling horses) since he heard he'd got the ride, to ensure he's in the best possible shape for the race. This is particularly good news bearing in mind that Klondike expects his jockeys to work every bit as hard as he does.

Oliver's already had his instructions from the Doc and there's more to come. Although it turns out that we all say much the same. Get off to a good start, keep up front if possible and don't give up – Klondike is likely to make up ground at the end as he's used to a longer trip. He pockets a note from Mr Byrne wishing him good luck, laughs when I say 'Remember to try and ENJOY it' and does the usual teenage thing of casting his eyes to heaven when his mother, naturally, tells him to 'take care'.

He heads off to do the things that proper jockeys do before they ride in a race. This starts in the dressing room where a valet has laid out the colours and helps him get dressed (not as essential for Oliver as he's only in one race but absolutely essential when jockeys are riding in consecutive races and have to stick to a strict timetable). Then he has a 'weigh in rehearsal'. He sits on the scales in the dressing room and checks his weight before heading off for the proper weighing room where his saddle and the appropriate lead weights are added to ensure he rides at the correct weight. He tells us later that the other jockeys have been helpful and supportive. The champion jockey, A. P. McCoy, makes a point of shaking his hand and wishing him well on his first ride in public.

We stand in the centre of the parade ring waiting for his reappearance. Klondike is looking as laid back as usual and Joe who's leading him round tries to get him to stretch out and walk more quickly. I notice that Klondike is a little over-dressed — his coat has grown and he's beginning to resemble a woolly bear. Horses are usually clipped for racing in the winter - it helps them deal with the sweating - but Klondike has escaped this (most horses seem to hate the very sound of the clippers) because he'll need his thick coat for his winter holiday in a field (which will start pretty much as soon as this race is over).

I look around at the other 'connections' in the ring. Nobody has turned out as a scruff but I'm pleased to see that our group looks particularly smart — as if we want to give all the support and encouragement that we can. We look professional. This is important business.

Oliver, who will break a few female hearts in the future, arrives and has obviously been well schooled in the courtesies of the parade ring. He walks in with confidence. He touches his cap and shakes hands with me and with horsey daughter as the owners. We play our part in carrying out the formalities without giggling or calling him 'Ollie'. Then he mounts the horse to calls of 'good luck, enjoy and come back safe.' Horsey daughter says 'Go for it' and his parents look as if he's heading for the scaffold.

As he goes down to the post, my greatest wish is that Mr Oliver

Dayman and Klondike Charger will come back unharmed and finish together! My greatest fear is that Colin will lose Ollie at the first and finish the race on his own. And it seems I wasn't the only one. The enormous cheer from our group when they successfully negotiated the first fence shocked the other owners round about us. Clearly we were demented and thought we'd won the race.

At every one of the 16 fences on the complicated figure of eight course, our hearts are in our mouths. At times it's a bit of a precarious partnership as Oliver learns his trade. Klondike, who knows his business well, is a forgiving animal and helps him by fiddling his way out of trouble. One horse falls and there are four in the race. There's a chance we could get in the frame, if only they can stay together. Oliver loses his whip but before it falls to the ground, manages to catch it again (the reflexes of a nineteen-year-old are extraordinary). The horse seriously clouts the fence five from home but somehow they stay together and the intake of breath from our group is audible to all. Heading down the home straight with three fences to jump they're lying third. Can they keep going? They can, they do and we drown out the shouts for the winner as we cheer them past the finishing post in third place. I look around the party. Smiles, jubilation and tears on every face – Dad included.

We run (thank God for sensible shoes) to cheer him into the third position in the winners' enclosure. He is mud-splattered and drunk with elation. He hugs the horse, thanks me over and over again for 'giving him the ride', hears congratulations from Mr Byrne on the mobile (much to the consternation of Teresa because of rules governing jockeys and mobiles at racecourses) and then heads off to handle the press.

They congratulate him and praise his riding. 'The horse is wonderful, helped me all the way. I couldn't have had a better birthday present' he tells them. I think he deserves his success – he's paid proper tribute to the horse. Nobody after all can do it without them.

Back at the lorry where we've gathered for Margot's fruit cake and sparkling wine (always on offer - win, lose or draw). I thank a soaking wet (thank heavens again for appropriate clothes) Klondike with a hug and a kiss on the nose for doing his bit and Oliver's parents thank me again and again for making it a 'very special day'.

Oliver arrives to walk the horse round (the Doc insists on an hour's walking to cool down before any horse heads off for home in the lorry). After the way he's handled the day I am sure one day Ollie will join the ranks of the professionals and he won't then be joining any inquests at the lorry. But for now, he just wants to savour the moment and that means being with his partner in glory. He also talks non-stop and we're treated to a run-down of every fence.

'Pinged the first, fantastic. Worried about the third but that was alright, nearly came off at the fourth ...we'd have got second if the race had been longer ...we were making up ground ...' His parents drink in every word, pride written all over their faces. He looks at his dad. 'Was that alright Dad?' Dad touches his arm. 'More than alright son.'

As we are about to head off for the long journey home, the thanks of jockey, parents and trainer's wife and mother for 'giving him the opportunity' are ringing in my ears and I feel guilty for my misgivings before the race when, I admit now, I worried that we were doing the right thing. One of our most successful horses in the hands of an absolutely green apprentice. Of course he had ridden him 'at home' but it's one thing to take well-known fences on a home gallop and quite another to jump sixteen you've never seen before, at full gallop with another four horses and riders battling for position. Injury is always possible to horse or jockey and this had been a risky venture.

Margot catches my elbow and with the wisdom of a mother of a jockey/trainer/racecourse doctor, says: 'Thank you for this. No matter how many races he rides in the future, no matter how many races he wins, THIS is the one he'll always remember.'

I call another 'well done' to Oliver and ask if he's celebrating his birthday and his ride at the pub tonight. He looks shocked. 'No way – I'm riding Red Emperor at Lingfield tomorrow, got to be fit for that.'

He's on his way.

So that was the equine – and human - drama at the track. But far from Fontwell another, connected, drama was unfolding. I hate missing seeing one of our horses run so I had plans to watch the race live in a bookie's shop.

The race was at 4 p.m. I left my home in Gloucestershire at around 12.45 on a journey which, depending on traffic, I was expecting to take around two-and-a-half hours.

Aargh No 1 came when I found myself (along with thousands of others) being guided off the M5 at the Cheltenham intersection by police barriers. The road was closed because of an accident.

You never know in this life when experience will come in handy. This time it was the hours spent in traffic jams in and around the hallowed ground of Prestbury Park during Festival time. I wouldn't claim to be a world expert in all the by-ways but I know more than a few and that knowledge came in handy as I made my way back on to the motorway at the Tewksbury turn-off.

That had cost me about 45 minutes but the motorway was clear and I whizzed through the dreaded M5/M6 connection at Wolverhampton and headed on down to Telford on the M54.

By 3 p.m. I was on the Telford ring road and half an hour later parking my car in Much Wenlock. I was congratulating myself on having arrived pretty much at the time I intended as I crossed a street to have a word with an elderly gentleman doing some gardening.

'Could you please direct me to the local bookies?' says I.

Aargh No 2 came with the reply 'It's just closed down.' I suspect I must have looked pretty agitated as I explained I wanted to get to a bookies so I could watch my horse run on television. 'If it's on television, you can watch it in my house' said my generous, new-found friend.

I somehow knew what the answer would be when I enquired whether he had satellite. It rapidly became obvious that the joys of At the Races let alone the wonders of SIS had somehow passed him by.

In the course of explaining to me just how to find the nearest bookies it also became obvious that my new friend was not only generous but also keen on detail. Left followed right, T junctions crowded in on third exits from roundabouts and the whole was rounded off with a 'It'll take about 15 minutes provided the traffic isn't too bad.' By now it's 3.40 p.m.

I was just about to flee, shouting my thanks but in truth not knowing whether at the first junction I should turn left or right let alone what happened 57 directions later when the elderly gentleman spotted a passing friend. The new chap said there was a bookies in a town closer. New but equally bewildering instructions followed and as I fled I had really grasped only two pieces of information.

The nearest bookies was in a place called Madeley and my new friend was quite clear. 'It's not a very nice place.' At this point I wouldn't have cared if it was Hades itself provided it had a betting shop that I could reach before four o'clock.

Aargh No 3 came at 3.50 when I ran from the car at the bottom of a hill having somehow found Madeley. I ran towards two middle-aged ladies. Panting I asked for the way to the nearest bookies. As the last syllables left my agitated lips I realised that these were very definitely ladies – but of the Chinese variety.

Now my Mandarin or indeed Cantonese is not the finest but as the machine gun delivery of a language I knew not splattered between them I decided to go for broke. 'Bookies' I said several times. Now neither actually said 'Ah so' but it was obvious that I had hit on a word (I suspect others might have included 'sweet' and 'sour') which they knew. With no words I understood but many gestures which I did, I was back in the car, up the hill and into the main town car park – thanking the legendary Chinese love of a gamble.

It was now 3.56 p.m.

Looking wildly round and spotting another lady standing at a bus stop I sped towards her.

Aagh No 4 came in response to my obvious question. This was a lady who obviously wanted to show off her expertise of a) Madeley; and b) the bookmaking options available . 'Well' she said, making herself more comfortable, 'there's two.'

Her description of the route to the first made the directions of my Much Wenlock friend seem a masterpiece of concision. I suspect I was a little less than polite when I interrupted her flow and said 'Just tell me the nearest.' As luck would have it, the nearest was just round the corner.

So it was at 3.58 p.m. that a red-faced, agitated, panting, overweight man in late middle-age burst into the local branch of Ladbrokes, the magic sign bookmakers. A dozen pair of eyes attached to bodies in seats occupied, I suspect, by the same people without fail every day, watched the stranger's agitated progress to place – just in time - a £20 loyalty bet on Colin and Ollie. They were still on me as I slumped into a chair just outside their magic circle and watched me breathing hard rather than the start of the four o'clock from Fontwell. This was a person they did not know, in Ladbrokes at four o'clock, interrupting their private club gathering. This unexpected event would no doubt be chewed over for some time.

The rest you know. By the time I had the quick mobile phone word with Ollie described earlier, I realised that I was all alone. Fontwell was the last race of the day. The regulars had departed leaving the stranger with no name (but definitely not Clint Eastwood) to the staff and the bank of brightly lit TV monitors.

But what was this? There was coverage of a race on one of them even if there seemed to be something not quite right about the pictures. The jerky movement of horses and riders suggested something seriously wrong in the transmission.

Then I realised I was watching, for the first time, virtual racing - computer generated images designed to keep the money flowing across the counters. Even when there's no satellite coverage of horse or dog meetings anywhere in the world, technology has come up trumps to make sure the dosh makes its time honoured journey from the punter's to the bookie's pocket.

I suddenly felt a warm affinity with the club members who had viewed me with such suspicion but had voted with their feet and left me to it as soon as the proper stuff was over. This is one private club which deserves to grow and prosper. Fancy anyone with more than two brain cells opting for make-believe when they can have the real drama of a young jockey like Ollie taking his first ride on a character like Colin.

That, Mr Ladbroke, is real magic.

Chapter

6

Terry Warner – the Owner's Owner

In over 40 years of owning horses, Terry Warner says he has only ever done it once. He'd always fancied having a grey horse and there was this one which had just finished third in a Saturday race at Chepstow.

He went over to the winners' enclosure to take a closer look and said – as you do—to nobody in particular 'What a lovely horse. I wouldn't mind buying him.' 'Well' said the chap nearest to him 'I happen to know he's for sale.'

And so the wheel of racing history turned. A check on the form showed that this 'nice, big strong horse' had won a little race at Taunton and been placed in several other bumpers and juvenile hurdles prior to his appearance at Chepstow. A chat with his trainer, Richard Mitchell, whose daughter Sophie had ridden the horse and whose wife was named as the breeder, revealed that he was indeed for sale – at a price of £60,000.

Now Terry Warner even on brief acquaintance gives the clear impression of a man not keen on over-paying. He offered £50,000. But when that offer was turned down with the information that several people were interested, Terry Warner showed another of the characteristics which you suspect have served him well. He made up his mind there and then and shook hands on the asking price. But there was one sensible proviso – 'subject to the vet.'

So the wheel of history had turned another degree. A

few days later, the vet went to the Mitchell yard in Devon. And back came the vet's opinion: 'Don't buy that horse. I can't get near him to scope him and check his wind.'

Now at this point the wheel could well have come off. But it did not. Terry Warner thought about it and decided that he had seen the horse on the racecourse. He had shown himself sound in limb and wind and he would back his own judgement.

So it was that this son of Riverwise (USA) by Came Cottage (Nearly a Hand), a grey gelding who'd been born on 1 April 1994, came to run in Terry Warner's yellow and black colours. His name: the not easily forgotten, Rooster Booster. He'd run off an official handicap mark of 114 that day at Chepstow on 11 March 2000. Three years later to the very day, on 11 March 2003, he stepped into the shoes just vacated by the mighty Istabraq and with a run which would see him rated 170 he won the Champion Hurdle. And one year later in the same race, he was 'carried out on his shield', as brave a second as we will see.★★

It was the first and only time that Terry had bought a horse like this - strictly on the basis of his own judgement. 'I suppose you could say that I have a one hundred per cent record.' In the process he gave the jumping public what it always seems to crave - a bold jumping grey who clearly relishes the sport. And with a name which is hard to forget.

For another, smaller but no less ardent group of National Hunt fans, he kept another dream alive. That one day, who knows, you might get to own a really serious horse.

You know money doesn't necessarily buy success and that's probably what keeps National Hunt racing going, the fact that you can be a relatively small owner like me and buy a Champion Hurdler for £60,000. Credit too to the Mitchell family who

---

★★ Cheltenham 2004 was Rooster Booster's second second on the trot. Two more seconds came at season's end in major races at Aintree and Punchestown.

bred him. You know he's English-bred and I don't think they've had the accolades they deserve.

You would be a very hard man indeed to begrudge Terry Warner and his wife, Jill their success. He owned his first horse, shared with two others, in 1963, just about the time Harold Macmillan was giving way to Sir Alec Douglas Home in the Prime Ministerial stakes. He had an interest in two or three horses every year until his retirement six years ago. That figure then went up to around 12 to 15, his long-promised retirement treat, one of them of course Rooster Booster whose Champion Hurdle win, he says, meant his 'lifetime ambition' in racing had been achieved.

But that win hasn't changed the habits of a lifetime. These days Terry still goes racing at his local tracks, two or three times a week —and that win hasn't diminished one jot the pleasure he gets in owning a winner.

The same week we won the Champion Hurdle we won a £20,000 race at Warwick - and we had nearly as much fun. The horse was Do L'enfant Deau. We'd bought him as a three-year-old from France. He turned out and won us six races in a season.

I think it's the elation of owning a winner. The elation of those few minutes is fantastic and hard to describe. Any winner gives you elation, even if it's a seller, you still get a lot of fun out of it. Of course if you go into the winners' enclosure at the big meeting at Cheltenham - which is like no other racecourse - well it is something again.

And the Warners have had that pleasure four times – twice with Rooster Booster and once each with Galileo and Kibreet.

But like many seeming fairy stories, once you penetrate the surface tougher elements appear. A few years ago, after a Cheltenham race Rooster Booster didn't win, the Warners were told by one of the top jockeys that he'd never win another hurdle race and we should go 'chasing with him'.

It so happened that that advice came when the Warners had lost two chasers on the racecourse in a fortnight. But Terry Warner went down to Somerset to see Rooster Booster schooled at Philip Hobbs' yard in Minehead. 'The horse didn't have a clue. He couldn't arch his back, he just wouldn't take to chasing. So I said to Philip that we shouldn't embarrass him by trying. The truth was, that after what had happened, I didn't want to risk losing another nice horse.'

So what does it feel like to lose two horses in a couple of weeks? 'Dreadful. You sort of curl up and die. You feel responsible for horse and jockey. It's rarely the jockey's fault when horses are killed. Everybody tries to console you – but really you want to be left alone and hide.'

It is the downside of racing – and part of it seems to be that it is the best horses who have the accidents because they're giving their all at the time. There's a risk every time you run. Every time I see a jockey get into the saddle of one of my horses I always say 'make sure you come back safe.' That's the biggest worry you have in all this, that the jockey and horse come back in one piece.

Even before that career crossroads for the horse, there had been another incident which had very nearly brought Terry Warner's racing story to an abrupt end – and this had nothing to do with accidents. This time it was the handicapper in the frame. About nine months after Rooster Booster had been bought he ran at Newbury, off a mark of 118. The distance was two miles and one furlong and the winners' prize money, £9,000.

Rooster Booster fell at the second last while in the lead. Next time out the horse had to carry an extra eleven pounds. Even from four years distance you can still feel Terry Warner's anger at the time when he spoke to the *Racing Post*.

> I put a lot of money into racing and have 15 horses in training. The fun goes out of it when the handicapper treats them like that. I feel like pulling out. We run them straight and get penalised for being honest

Looking back, Terry admits he was very incensed and came very close to quitting 'Time and time again we see a horse 20 lengths clear fall at the last or second last and the handicapper puts him up. But often, even if they're at the last hurdle and look certain to win, they get beaten on the run in.'

So what stopped him giving up? With a smile he says that he had just retired 'and I didn't know what I was going to do with all my spare time.' Some of that time these days is spent in taking a keen interest in the handicapping system. Before one of his horses race he says that he will spend most of the previous day working his way through the form book. He has that kind of mathematical brain. So it's with that understanding that he takes the handicapper to task over another matter.

> It is wrong that the horse that comes second in a race is put up only a couple of pounds less than the winner. There should be a greater difference. Every horse should be allowed to win one race in its career.

All these considered thoughts from a lifetime in racing ownership are uttered in the unvarnished and unmistakable tones of Terry Warner's home county of Gloucestershire. In fact he now lives in a house not far from the A38 and just five miles away from the farm on which he was born and brought up.

He does almost appear to have come into the world 71 years ago with one very clear idea. Whatever else he was going to do with his life he was not going to follow his father and generations of Warners before him and continue farming.

Jill and Terry Warner either side of Rooster Booster, winner of the 2003 Champion Hurdle and a gallant second in 2004 (Photo © Grossick Photography).

It seemed to me to be a lot of hard work, seven days a week, for a not very good return. And let's face it, I would never have had racehorses if I'd gone farming.

At 16 he left school with no qualifications at all. A job had been lined up with a local auctioneers. The long summer months stretched ahead and with Terry's antipathy towards farm work well known he was asked-bluntly one suspects – how he was going to fill his time. There was a job advertised in the local paper for a temporary junior sales assistant in a sports shop in Gloucester.

Terry liked it and so was lost forever to the world of auctioneering. He was just nineteen when the buyer for the shop left. Terry's nearness to hand won over any misgivings

about his youth. He got the job. It meant he knew the trade inside out, more than useful when, at the age of 29, he decided to strike out on his own.

Rooster Booster with Richard Johnson winning the 2003 Champion Hurdle (Photo © Grossick Photography).

The best place for his venture, he decided, was in a shop directly opposite the one he was leaving. 'A bit tense' is how he describes his last few weeks. And it doesn't sound as if there was much of a do to mark his departure. 'Their parting words were that they would break me in three months.'

Suffice it to say they didn't and by the time the business was sold there were 22 shops throughout the West Country and the Midlands which bore the legend *Terry Warner Sports* above the door. The shops sold the whole range of sports goods but the word is that it was the mania for trainers which really made the Warner fortune. It is the word too that when the business was sold he was richer by several million pounds. He politely declines the opportunity to be more specific. And why should he? This was a business with no shareholders, no partners and no bank loans.

What his farmer father would have made of it all heaven literally knows. He died many years before Terry sold out. 'He couldn't understand why I wanted to open a second shop. That's farmers I suppose. They can be a bit negative. In any business if you don't grow it you go backwards.'

On the way Terry had a series of horses which obviously gave him the pleasure of ownership but with some sound commercial sense mixed in as well. Warner for Leisure, Warner for Players and Warner for Sports all won. In the process of having fun, the horses advertised the business. 'I never had more than one at a time. But it got us on the telly and people associated the horses with the business. They would come into the shops and ask about them.'

Those horses were unbroken stores so that he could name them to his advantage. 'It was all much more long term. These days, now that I'm older, I buy horses with proven form, off the flat or at the sales. I have to say that I think French horses are the best value these days. The Irish can now afford to keep the best horses for themselves.'

As you become more successful I think you tend to try to upgrade your horses and try and buy a better horse with better form in the first place. I have paid over £100,000 for three of my horses. They've all won but there are no guarantees. And all of them - with one notable exception - have been bought through agents.

A heart attack at around 60 – 'it must have been stress I suppose' - made him think and he sold out five years later 'as it turned out, at the top of the market.' He and Jill ('she's not as keen as me but she likes to be there when we have our own runners') have been married 42 years and have produced two children who in turn have had three grandchildren. One of the boys has more than caught Grandpa's eye. Five–year-old Jack is 'nuts on racing. He knows all our horses and pretty well everybody's colours. He's good about the jockeys too.'

These days, the grandchildren, racing and the doings of the handicapper, as well as an interest in commercial property, keep him busy. And in the summer, on the 20 acres that surround their property, usually 8 to 10 of the horses come for their summer holidays.

Currently there are 11 wholly owned horses, and five owned in partnerships. Because he has been a successful owner with well over 200 winners so far, friends ask him to join and 'it's hard to say no'. But for a partnership to succeed, he says, 2 to 3 people works best.

When it comes to trainers, nobody could accuse him of not giving people a go. Currently Warner horses are in the care of Philip Hobbs, Paul Nicholls, Alan King, Ian Williams, Tom George, David Gandolfo and Barry Llewellyn. As well as the horses already named, the wholly owned include: Andy Gin, Majlis, Bacardi Boy, Brooklyns Gold, Nagamo, Roosters Reunion and Random Guest. Part owned include Sud Bleu, Cobreces, Bourbon Manhattan, and Giant's Rock.

He has had horses with Philip Hobbs the longest – he has provided over half his winners tally – and he would have more. But Hobbs' law applies to everyone, even people who bring a Champion Hurdler into the yard. Nobody is allowed to have more than four animals at any one time because if there should be a falling out it would leave too big a gap.

Philip Hobbs is probably the most dedicated guy in racing. His whole life is racing. He eats, sleeps and drinks racing. He's so dedicated he has to be successful. And his wife is a very good back-up. His communications are probably better than any other trainer going. He will phone you once or twice a week, at least, when you have horses running. And he keeps you informed. Even when they're not running he lets you know what's going on.

Compliments too for the Hobbs jockey and regular pilot of Rooster Booster, Richard Johnson. 'He's first class and he's a very nice, personable lad too. I think it is unfortunate from his point of view that's he's been riding in the same era as Tony McCoy, otherwise he would have been champion jockey – something I hope he will achieve in due course. He's entitled to it.'

Over forty years as an owner has meant that Warner has seen quite a few changes in the sport he clearly loves.

When I first came into it an owner was nothing, you weren't recognised, you were just there. Now racecourses treat you much better and things have improved dramatically, particularly in the last few years.

But what does amaze me is the way the press don't want to know the owners. All they're interested in is the trainer. In fact the trainer gets more ego than the owners ever get. Trainers really are little Gods. It's funny when you read about your horse in the papers, it's trainer this and trainer that. You can't help thinking: 'Well, what have I done?' And what you've done is lay all the money out. He may well be a wonderful trainer but he still needs somebody to find the horses for him. Owners aren't thought of highly enough.

I think people coming in now as owners are coming in much more for the ego. And I don't see anything wrong in that.

There is a word of caution for those new people coming in. 'There's an awful lot of wheeling and dealing in the horse business. A lot of people make fortunes out of horses. I think that owners do pay through the nose overall, there's no doubt about that. We do get tucked up a treat. You do have to live on your wits with it really.'

And so to questions of money. Has he made money from the sport? 'I did in the year when we won the Champion Hurdle – but that was the first and only time. But it's a hobby and you expect to pay for a hobby.'

And gambling? 'It's not a huge part of the whole. I do like a gamble – but I'm a £30 a race person. Twice in my life I have laid £1,000 on a horse. So it's not going to affect my lifestyle – but I do have a yen to beat the bookies. I see that as a challenge.'

As for the future of the sport, Terry Warner is optimistic. 'I think all the tracks will survive. There's room for them all really. Certainly I didn't like the idea Cheltenham came up with, that the small courses should lose all their big races which could then be concentrated on the big tracks. I think Exeter, Huntingdon and the rest should have their big days. That's what keeps them going. I think it's a dreadful idea.'

For understandable reasons you can't talk horses and racing with Terry Warner for long without returning to the horse who, for entirely understandable reasons, is the apple of both his eyes. Rooster Booster will hopefully be back for several more summers to take the Gloucestershire air but when he's there he doesn't put on a champion's airs and graces. 'When we have ten of them with us, he'll be the last one to get his feed. He lets the others argue over the piles of food and then he takes whichever is left. He's very laid back.'

Except in that one respect which might have made many another prospective owner think twice – that matter of the vet's scope. To this day Rooster Booster still thinks he has a clean record in that regard. But he hasn't. They had to knock him out to do it but he was scoped only once, just before he won the Champion Hurdle.

But surely Rooster Booster has earned his delusion, just as Terry Warner is entitled to his spot in the sun after a lifetime in the sport. After all, he's a man who earned it by trusting his own judgement.

Chapter 7

David's Diary 3

NOVEMBER 29

It was one of those days. The rain never stopped and the only variant was when the downpour was caught by the cold wind. No matter what you wore or what you were doing, if you were outside you got both wet and cold. And no, I hadn't just momentarily stepped out of the warmth of an owners' and trainers' bar into a parade ring. Here I was, trying to be a good Dad, doing a stint helping my daughter whose normal Saturday help had been called to mock GCSE torture.

As I am sure all stable staff would agree, it does us owners no harm at all to shovel the brown stuff when wet through having risen at 6.30 a.m. sharp to enjoy the privilege. I am actually in the stable of the third horse in our party, Gloster Gunner. He is only four but that digit is the only small thing about him. Already he stands seventeen hands high and every time I see him I utter the same prayer: 'Please Gunner - stop growing.'

As the name suggests, he is out of Gunner B, the legendary stallion who produced so many decent National Hunt horses. He was legendary in more ways than one. He was still serving mares when he passed away aged 29 with - I hope - a smile on his face. Gloster Gunner, who is the bright chestnut colour so often associated with his sire, was among the last of the breed.

In the best traditions of the gentle giant, he is as easy a horse to handle in the stable as you could wish. You can

Gloster Gunner and Oliver Dayman, both hopes for the future.

move him round as you wish, always allowing that he will give you the occasional nuzzle and a face full of warm nostril-driven air as you go about your business. His good nature is just as well because the Gunner's toilet habits leave a little to be desired. Not for him the neat habits of some. He is a disciple of the 'trample it in and see how far we can then spread it' school.

Gunner with David Crosse in the parade ring at Doncaster.

Despite the wind, the rain and the hard work I have to admit I actually enjoy getting this close to horses. My age and bulk mean I can't ride them so this is the next best way of getting to know them and their characters. And of course, as any stable staff are more than entitled to point out long and loud, I don't have to do it every day.

My daughter's seven-box yard is on a farm near Lechlade on the Gloucestershire-Oxfordshire border and it's here the horses have their holidays and are prepared to go in to full training. We have a special but not unique relationship. I pay her to have the horses but, being a Dad, receive nothing for my labours.

It's a good hour's drive both there and back from my home, so I can only go about once a week. When she was closer I was much more of a regular, turning up two or three times a week. Some days - when I get really lucky - I get to muck out five or six stables - and go home trying not to look too grateful for the sit-down in the car. But at least I can look the stable staff in the eye when I meet them at the races.

These people really are the unsung heroes and heroines of the sport. The money has improved but the hours are long and the job can be tough so it really is good to see them get some kind of recognition on race days. Well done to the courses who, for big races, are printing their names next to their horses in the racecards. Credit too, to the people who are making sure the staff get in on the act on the winners' rostrum. Good also to see the TV companies these days making sure that the people who do so much of the work getting horses fit and well get the recognition they deserve. And a final credit to Martin Pipe, champion trainer fourteen times but not always the most popular man in the sport. Just watch how the champion trainer makes sure his staff get in on the photographs on big race days. Sure the owners pay the bills but it's the staff who do the graft. It's their big day too with their horse. It's an example other trainers could follow.

You will notice I have called them 'staff'. I never know whether to laugh or cry when you see some gnarled veteran looking old enough to be even my grandfather being described as a 'lad'. You can take these things too far but titles do matter.

Gloster Gunner has not long come out of a field which he had shared at various times with our other racehorses. Like most horses, Gunner doesn't like being on his own. More recently his companion has been a Shetland pony by the name of Mini Me. And quite a sight they have made, creating their own equine version of the odd couple.

Mini Me is as short and round as Gunner is tall and gangly. At first my daughter thought the Shetland was pregnant but as she refuses to be caught and month follows month with nothing transpiring, it was decided that the roundness was simply the way she is. There are those of us who understand.

Gunner will now spend about four or so weeks starting from walk and going up to fast canter before he goes into full training at the Doc's. He ran just once the previous season in a bumper at Newton Abbot. They're the prep races for young jumping horses where they get to go to the races, adjust to the crowds and the noise but without the added complications of jumping obstacles.

Officially they are called National Hunt flat races but our Irish cousins – whose invention they were – called them bumpers for the simple reason that as the horses go round the bends they bump into each other. When you think about it, there aren't too many curving running rails to adjust to in the wide-open spaces.

Frankly I am dubious about the whole business but short of running them straight over hurdles there aren't too many options. Bumpers tend to be run as the last race on the card and usually attract bumper fields. So in the gathering gloom you get twenty and more green young horses charging around, jockeys hanging on for grim death, as they collide with each other. Is it any wonder that the safety record in these races leaves a lot to be desired.

Added to this, many of the horses who have failed in flat yards are sent to get experience in bumpers. So muddled up with National Hunt horses like Gloster Gunner, born and bred to be a steeplechaser, you have got failed speed merchants who only a few months before were being talked about as potential Derby winners. It is an odd mixture.

Steps have been taken to create age categories and vary the minimum distances but more needs to be done. Of course things aren't helped by the fact that there are people who make good money from bumpers. You get a reasonable young horse, over-train it to win a bumper, and then sell it on at a fancy price. Let's remember the original idea was to provide a genuine development experience for horses bred to tackle steeplechases and for whom hurdling may not be the right route.

Like Jessie MacDougall, Gloster Gunner is co-owned with Terry and Lilian in the Four for Fun partnership and, again like her, is the product of the breeding operation we had with our previous partners. You can't help feeling that extra closeness to the ones you breed. To a degree you play God, picking father and mother. When the big day comes, within hours you are at the foaling stable as leggy newborn is shown off by the proud if exhausted mother.

That's the storybook version. The reality with Gunner was that he had surely the worst case of knock knees ever seen on a foal quite that tall and skinny. Of course for the first few months a foal's knees are all out of proportion. Usually it is a characteristic to make people go *aah* but in Gunner's case it was plain worrying. The legs splayed in a perfect *v*, topped off with two huge knees, almost but not quite hiding the frankly soppy look he wore at all times in those days.

We fretted and worried and were given all kinds of advice by vets and others. At one point an operation looked the only hope – but in the end we took the advice of an old hand and let nature take its course. The end result – legs as straight as you could wish. The end of worries on that count then? Not a bit of it.

Horses' cannon bones are the ones that connect – in human terms – the knee and the ankle. They are also where, for jumping horses, the all-important front tendon runs – the one that takes a lot of the strain as the horse takes off and lands. I am no vet (perhaps it was lack of those science subjects) but I know enough to know that some experts think that for steeplechasers the shorter the cannon bone (and therefore the tendon) the better. There is quite simply less to go wrong.

Step forward Gloster Gunner, whose beautifully straight legs would do a West End dancer proud. Some trainers would argue with such cannon bones he will inevitably get problems and therefore it is best if he does something other than become a racehorse. Others say that such horses should be fired – a somewhat grisly process that involves creating scar tissue . And still others say that all horses are different – worry when you have a problem and not before.

I was the one fretting and Terry and self have talked endlessly about what to do. In the end the Doc, who is the horse's trainer, advised us to do nothing and let Gunner take his chance. He is what he looks – a big weak horse who will run only a few times this season but hopefully the training and time at the racecourse will come in useful in a couple of years' time. That's the way that Gunner B's foals usually go and if he is half as good as some of them we will be well-satisfied.

He has caused us problems in one other area. Here I must declare an interest. To begin with, before he was named officially or otherwise, he was called 'Snippet', never, I thought, the most appealing of nomenclatures. He was born in Gloucestershire, home of the Royal Gloucestershire Regiment who fought so bravely in, among other campaigns, Korea and gained the sobriquet 'Glorious Glosters' at the battle of Imjin. Why not, I suggested, Gloster Gunner? The others agreed and he was so-named.

By the time we got to the Doc's we all just called him Gunner. It was then the delightful Emily, aged 17, and in her first job, intervened. 'Gunner B', she mused to herself, 'that rhymes with Bumble Bee.' And so it was that before we knew it people were saying to us 'Bumble looks well.' Why, I have wondered to myself, if a stable name was needed, didn't someone take up the opportunity to accurately call the horse 'Gee-Gee'?

I have tried sarcasm ('If I'd wanted something out of bloody Mrs Tiggywinkle …'), black looks and heavy sighs – but I fear I am wasting my time. But if anybody thinks that as he jumps the last just before a winning run up the

Cheltenham Hill I shall be among those shouting 'Come on BUMBLE' well, they have another think coming.

DECEMBER 5

This day finds me at Gatwick Airport – and Jessie MacDougall due to run in the Marian Peett Juvenile Novices' Hurdle at Sandown Park. What's more Jessie is running from the stable of the Doc and not, as previously, from David Evans' yard.

After Jessie's Saturday October 4th run at Chepstow we were told on the Monday that all was well. Two days later came news of a minor problem in her back. There then followed quite a few weeks of frustration in which it was hard to tell what was going on. Not even his best friends could describe David as one of the great communicators and his split from his wife Debbie – who is now training on her own account – has meant that he is trying to cover a lot of ground on his own.

We had agreed between us that Terry would deal with David to keep it simple for the trainer and because I was already dealing with two trainers on my own account. Over the next few weeks my partner's frustration was becoming ever more obvious. His attempts to get hold of David were only rarely successful and we were never absolutely clear whether or not the horse was in full or light work and quite what the problem was.

Eventually it was agreed that she would be entered in a juvenile novices' hurdle at Hereford in November. Then, just a few minutes before the overnight declarations were due to close, Terry got a call to say the horse was not right and couldn't run.

We then decided – with trainer Evans' agreement – to let Teresa Pritchard, whose skills as a back doctor we have learned to trust over the years, take a look. So we shipped the horse to the Doc's yard. The result: a diagnosis which said the back was fine, it was her feet that were the problem.

We then decided the horse could stay where she was.

At the time of writing, a negotiated settlement is – I hope - about to be agreed about some outstanding money matters. These things happen in life and in racing but I'd like to think that in the not too distant future Terry, self and David Evans will be able to raise a glass at a racecourse. He is certainly not on my list of people I would rather never set eyes on again and I shall not forget that he produced Jessie to win her very first race at Haydock Park at 33/1.

Which brings us to Gatwick Airport. In my business career I did more than my share of flying as the one million BA air miles in my account bear witness. Like everyone else, hopping from one continent to another, you fervently pray that delays will be avoided. Well, not this day at Gatwick.

My flight to Italy to see my brother and his wife - he's lived there since 1967 - had been long-planned. The time scales which racing brings to the diary sometimes mean for the sake of staying on-side with family and friends that racing has to take second place. So it was for this trip. However that still left a little room to manoeuvre.

The flight was scheduled to leave at 1.35 p.m.- and the race would be off at 1.30 p.m. Just this once, a half hour delay would be absolutely fine. This would allow me to at least to watch the race on satellite TV in the BA club lounge, provided, of course, I could persuade my fellow loungers that the 1.30 at Sandown was rather more important than the world news which is the staple diet usually on offer.

Internet apart, following your horses when you are abroad is no easy matter. My experiences have included odd scenes at odd hours in Sri Lanka and Australia and once in the back of a cab in Budapest. There you are, mobile phone pressed to ear as a primed friend back in the UK has held their phone in the general direction of the At the Races coverage or a speaker phone with the live telephone commentary.

As it turned out my return flight was a hour late in taking off (and because of fog we were diverted to Bournemouth) but the outward flight, the one that mattered in Sandown terms, was called spot on time. Now you are allowed to use mobiles (on which I could listen to the live commentary) until they start the engines but I could see that it was going to be very tight for my particular schedule.

Flight crews are no different to the rest of us. There are cheery ones and grumpy ones. There are even racing fans among them. This lot seemed quite cheerful so I took my chances, went up to the front of the plane at 1.25 and explained my problem, beginning with the well-worn words 'Now you know you get people making daft requests...'. One of the stewardesses took more than average interest. What was the horse called etc. I had found my fan. And through the open door to the flight deck I noted that the pilot had also heard my plea.

Obviously when they had to start the engines they would need to do so to meet the flight take-off slot - but they wouldn't do so before they had to. I returned to my seat thinking I had a chance. When the captain came on the p.a. system to do the usual announcements and completed it by saying ' ... and we've had a request not to start the engines too soon'. I knew I would at least hear the race.

It has to be said that we had no great hopes for success for Jessie in this particular contest. She had been off the track for 62 days, with worries over both back and feet plus the fact that she had been through the disruption of moving yards. Normally a voracious eater, she had been much less hoover-like of late, something which could well be to do with her getting used to a new routine in a new place.

Why run her then? Simply because she needs three runs to get a proper handicap over hurdles. She had seemed fine and schooled well. This would be the second of three runs in what are in effect level weight contests, penalties for winners and fillies' allowance apart. How else can the handicapper make a fair assessment?

Agent Dave Roberts offered five jockeys for the race. After a chat with Terry we opted for Jason Maguire, Tom George's stable jockey. He has ridden a variety of horses for us over the years and we knew he would do as we would ask – let the horse take her chance without putting her under unnecessary pressure.

Fortunately, as I re-fastened my seat belt, the mobile phone signal couldn't have been better as the starter called in the seven horses for the minimum trip of two miles, with Jessie as a perfectly fair 33/1 and carrying my loyalty bet of £20 each way (when she had won at Haydock – at the same price – Mrs Byrne and I had precisely £5 each way between us).

These kind of juvenile novices' hurdle races are not that easy to find, so we had decided to crack on and run her even though on flat form ratings there were several way above her in class. For the first circuit and a bit on good to soft ground, Jessie was in the leading bunch but as they started to quicken she was rapidly going backwards, finishing last, beaten 30 lengths by the winner.

My later viewing of a recording of the race confirmed that her lack of racing had meant that she couldn't go the pace. Even though she was never even going to get placed, her previous form would have had her a lot closer. But that was later. On the aircraft, I held up my hand as soon as the race was over and sure enough as I pressed the off button on my phone the engines started.

'How did she do?' asked the stewardess later and I explained. But that wasn't quite the end of the story. As I was leaving the aircraft and saying a genuine thank you to the cabin crew for their help the stewardess handed me a folded sheet which she said was a little present. Handling various bags and coats I said more thanks and slipped the paper into my inside jacket pocket – and then forgot all about it.

It was some days later, near the finish of a seriously decent three-hour, three-bottle lunch with my brother in a fish restaurant in Trieste, that my hand, looking for a pen in my inside jacket pocket found instead a sheet of paper. What was this?

Opening it out, I found a page torn from a magazine. In purple and yellow silks a frustrated looking professional jockey was pictured trying to achieve some forward momentum on a very small grey donkey which had clearly been left at the start. It made me laugh out loud. Of course I saw the joke. After all, Jessie is black not grey.

DECEMBER 11

'Why do we put ourselves through this?' The question came from a rather white-faced Mrs Byrne. And it is a question which could be asked of any of the owners featured in this book – including this one – without, I suspect, getting an entirely satisfactory answer.

The question was posed at Huntingdon racecourse, a track which is one of the diminishing number to which we had never been before. The reason for breaking our duck was the seasonal reappearance of Burwood Breeze, a seven-year-old trained by Tom George in the lovely Gloucestershire village of Slad, made famous by Laurie Lee in his memoir *Cider With Rosie*.

Breeze is the fourth and final member of the quartet of horses which currently dominate our lives and is owned by wife and self. We bought him as an unraced five-year-old for £15,000 through Tom from his father-in-law John Edwards, who used to train in the Wye valley but is now Irish-based.

Breeze is by a US sire and ran with moderate success for a season as a hurdler (although he is very much bred as a three mile steeplechaser with Welsh and Scottish National winners in his dam's pedigree). Then last season, as a novice 'chaser', he had come second at Plumpton, Newcastle and Perth in his last three outings.

'A workman-like gelding' is how *Chasers and Hurdlers* described him and even with an owner's biased eye it would be hard to disagree. He seems to have grown out of his earlier habit of whipping round without warning and ditching whoever happened to be on his back, and so adding a fiver each time to the Christmas party fund which operates at Tom's stables.

In fact he is one of nature's decent sorts, easy to handle in the stable and a trier. There are worse combinations.

He is now the finished article and Tom has said several times how he has clearly matured over the summer and although he won't win many beauty parades, he brings some useful extras besides looks to the table. First of all he can still run in novice races even though he has quite a bit of experience and knows his way round. Second, he is off an official handicap mark of 96 – even though his Postmark is 110 and Timeform rate him 98. His third attribute is, despite making the odd mistake, a real ability to jump steeplechase fences. Truth to tell we still don't know quite what we have got with Breeze and, as Tom says, we won't really be certain until the end of this season. Hard not to create a little extra saliva as I write that.

This race at Huntingdon and a non-handicap at Taunton had both been entered at the five-day stage and it took only a couple of seconds to decide the Fenland course was the one for us. Some pretty fancy youngsters were due to run in Somerset on ground officially good to firm. Our chap proved he could handle good ground as well as the softer stuff at the back end of last season but serious good to firm is definitely not for him. Also a non-handicap brings us back to level weights contests.

Next we came to the question of jockeys. Tom is never keen to run two horses in the same race, but with the lack of water still causing problems he explained that he would have to include Drom Wood in the line-up at Huntingdon. That gave stable jockey Jason Maguire a problem. When

Tom asked what I wanted to do I said I would let Jason make the choice and no hard feelings. He has put a lot of work at home into both horses and for various reasons had missed two recent wins on Drom Wood.

Tom went off to discuss his options with Jason and he was quite a while in coming back. Jason, it transpired, was finding it tough to make a decision and didn't want to upset anyone. Having my assurance that I wouldn't be upset, Jason opted for Drom Wood, on the grounds that he was fully fit and our chap was having his first run. Fair enough, and I agreed with Tom that we would give the ride to Robert 'Chocolate' Thornton who had been Breeze's partner in a hurdle race at Taunton and was currently lying fourth in the jockeys' table.

In track terms, Huntingdon put me in mind of a right-handed Newbury on a smaller scale, open and flat with decent fences offering a fair test. I can't say the facilities were in the same class. There was something of the 1960s about the place.

The Tote Credit club revealed an early price of 9/2 against Breeze. I decided that I was unlikely to do much better than that so had my main bet of £250 on the nose at that price.

On arrival at the saddling stall we found Tom and his box driver saddling up with Alice, the girl who looks after Breeze and rides him every day, holding his head. We'd met before when I'd been on a stable visit and she confessed to feeling really excited to be with Breeze on his first outing of the season. She's a nice girl and it is good to see enthusiasm like that in any young person - particularly, it has to be said, when it is directed at your horse.

Tom lifted up the horse's cover to show us how fit the horse was looking and then said that Jason now thought he might have made the wrong choice. Wry smiles and shoulder shrugs.

In the parade ring, with no Drom Wood connections present, Jason joined up with Tom and Chocolate plus the

Byrnes. I could see Jason was a bit uncomfortable so I congratulated him on an excellent win for the George stable in the second on the card. I had had a reasonable bet and that, plus another winner, meant the cash reserves were several hundred to the good. I could see he was glad that I really didn't bear any grudge.

Of course there was sport to be had so I turned to Chocolate and said: 'The instructions for this race are dead simple. Whatever else we have to finish in front of him,' pointing at Jason. I got my smile and for good measure I wished both jockeys 'good luck and come back safe.' I then headed for the bookies' ring, where I found Breeze and Drom Wood joint favourites at 7/2, with Breeze threes in places. With my earlier winnings burning a hole in my pocket I bet another £100 on Breeze at 7/2 while taking

Alice, Burwood Breeze and the author at Bangor where, after 18 visits to the racetrack and 6 seconds, the horse broke his duck.

some smug satisfaction in the 9/2 early bird bet.

And so to the race. We were delighted by Breeze's jumping; he was spot on taking a length or two out of the others at just about every fence. He was second for most of the race and as they were about half a mile from home he was urged on by 'Chocolate' to close the gap with the leader. At first he looked to be gaining but then his lack of recent races told. Course commentator Derek Thompson had just said 'And Burwood Breeze looks set for second for the fourth time on the trot' when it happened.

The *Racing Post* analysis put it like this '...(an) exhausted Burwood Breeze shook his head approaching the last and went to pull up before clambering over and subsiding on landing when 20 lengths down but well clear of the rest.'

Frankly, through the glasses it was hard to tell immediately what had happened with the final fence hard to our right. All we knew for sure was that our horse had gone down and not got up. We immediately started to cut through the crowd to get to him. The memories came flooding back – our hurdler, Hubert, who looked as if he would have to be shot at Chepstow with a cracked pelvis and who never raced again. And then there was Polydamas, who collapsed and died at the same track in the unsaddling enclosure immediately after a race.

But this was the first time we had seen the dreaded green screens starting to go up round one of our horses. We could also see that Chocolate was sitting on top of the fallen horse. I had a clear picture of Richard Dunwoody doing the same at Wincanton when it was obvious in mid-air that the poor creature had broken its back. The other picture that remained in the memory was of the distress of the ten or eleven-year-old girl who was, I reckoned. the daughter of the owner.

All that went on in my head as we half ran and stumbled towards the fence. And then – thank God – the whole picture changed. The screens were down and the horse was up, unsteady and clearly winded, but up. The jockey had done a great job keeping the horse on the ground so stopping him, frightened and breathless, doing much more lasting damage to himself.

Breeze was quickly led away – best to keep him moving, said Tom – and Chocolate had to rush away to weigh in and to ride in the next race which, in the way of National Hunt racing, he won.

It takes a while for the head to clear and the emotions to settle after that kind of incident. And it was then Mrs Byrne asked her question. Just why do we put ourselves through it? I guess, being honest, because the thrill of this kind of sport comes partly because of the danger to the horses and riders. And of course because – speaking personally – I love it. Never is my mind clearer and more concentrated than when watching one of our horses compete. Of course the last thing you want is the kind of scene we had just witnessed – but it is part of the sport and if anyone can't accept it (while hating it with every fibre of your being) well, it is best they take an interest in something else. Horses fall and some of them get killed or injured.

The bravery, honesty and sheer decency of horses is quite extraordinary. Breeze had literally run to his last breath because he was asked to, he had given until there was nothing more to offer. The deal, as Jenny Pitman said, is that horses get to live in the equivalent of a five-star hotel. In return we ask them to race their best for us. It would be a hard man who judged that Breeze hadn't kept his side of the bargain on December 11th.

In hindsight, as we ran in rings to try and avoid a firm surface and finished up on good to soft ground at Huntingdon, we would have been better off over two and a half miles first time out. Hindsight eh? In case you are wondering, Drom Wood was pulled up by Jason before the second last.

As we were leaving the track I decided I couldn't leave without checking on the horse – and Alice. Security at the racecourse stables were understanding and took trouble to get me signed in and round to his stable. Back to the door and still a little trembly there he was. Alice was with him and had clearly been through exactly the same emotions as the owners ('our' horse shared in triumph and disaster 'just the same').

If Breeze could have spoken I am sure he would have said 'It's not fair' and was there just a hint of a jutting lower lip? But then he got his eye on me. Remember I had cleared his stable many a time at my daughter's and led him to and from the field. Little treats - away from my daughter's sight - were part of the process.

Suddenly his eye took on a different cast and he nuzzled my left pocket. There, somewhere battered and not entirely without the benefit of some fuzz, were two very old polo mints. Once they were safely in his mouth both eyes closed as the serious slurping got underway.

The last part of the *Racing Post* analysis concerning Breeze said '…he got up and walked away and considering this was his first run for 210 days on softening ground, he was far from disgraced and if none the worse for the experience, can make amends.'

Amen to that. Perhaps I'll read it out to him when I go and wish him Merry Christmas. But I think I'll give him the polo mints first.

Chapter
8

Jim Lewis - Lucky Jim

As someone has observed: 'There's lucky, there's very lucky – and then there's Jim Lewis.' You'd have to be seriously uninterested in racing not to have become familiar with the man with a shock of white hair and the toothbrush moustache which tops off a grin as big as they come. The reason for that beam: the horses he's pictured leading into winning spots are those about which most of us can only dream.

This 70-year-old is of course the owner of Best Mate, Edredon Bleu, Impek, Nakir and several more. Matey, winner of an incredible three Cheltenham Gold Cups and a King George; Blue, winner of one of the great Queen Mother Champion Chases when he beat Direct Route and now also a winner of the King George. If all that was not enough, Lewis has picked up the trophies for an Arkle, a Grand Annual Chase, three Haldon Gold Cups, five Peterborough Chases and the Erricson Chase in Ireland. Little wonder then, if you spot him at the races, you see he has become something of a star in his own right.

All sports needs their heroes. In racing, rightly, the four - legged friends take the laurels, closely followed by the top trainers and jockeys. But jump racing could do a lot worse than have an owner like Jim Lewis in the spotlight. He exudes a joy in the success of his horses which you can almost touch. But it's balanced by his obvious willingness to share the success. If you want to believe for an afternoon or a race that Matey or Blue is yours, he says why not?

There's a part of National Hunt racing that does belong to everybody. You see the crowds, the vast majority are never going to have a horse of their own. As far as I'm concerned, they can share mine. I want them to enjoy the sport and feel they belong.

This from the working class kid made good; the ordinary punter who's been part of the crowd, dreaming of one day owning a tiny piece of a horse; then the owner who had his share of losers as he trailed round the gaff tracks. His whole story is one which bears more than a passing resemblance to a fairy tale. The ordinary Jim who made it all the way – and beyond. And still a man who, far away from the glamour of Cheltenham, Sandown or Leopardstown, takes his wife for an afternoon's racing at Worcester or Hereford.

I met him at his home in a village, a few miles from Worcester. It's a nice comfortable, unpretentious bungalow in an acre of garden and with a water feature – he explains before we go into the house – paid for from Edredon Bleu's winnings in that wonderful Champion Chase..

Once inside, trophies and mementoes occupy just about every shelf. In fact there's so many, there's no room for spotlights picking out individual prizes. The Gold Cups, side by side, get no more nor less space than the others.

Here you meet the other major character in this romance, his wife of 47 years, Valerie. She is as Brummie and friendly as her husband – and like most long-married couples they can obviously finish each other's sentences and think each other's thoughts. There is, too, that sense of understanding you get from people who together have faced whatever life has thrown at them.

In a way, it was Valerie who set them off on a journey which gives the lie to the delusion that without a good middle class home and a university degree you might as well not bother.

There they were, he 16 and she 14, standing on a hill overlooking the old Bromford Bridge racetrack in Birmingham. It was a local courting spot and so the young couple were only partly there because they hadn't the money to pay to get into the racing taking place below.

With his arm around her, Jim said 'One day, when we're married, I'll buy you a house, and we'll have a Jaguar car; and a racehorse.' The response from the girl who Jim's Dad had already told him was 'too posh for us' shows, even at the age of 14, a sense of the practicalities of life which have no doubt served the couple well. 'Get off with you' she said.

It was not Jim's first contact with the racetrack. As a nine-year-old he was a paperboy and the racecourse was part of his round. On race days, the turnstiles were a welcome sight. There he could unload quantities of the old *Sporting Life* and the long-gone *Sporting Buff*, making his bag a whole lot lighter.

He remembers watching the charabancs arriving for the meeting and parking in the streets around his home. The young Lewis was fascinated by the names of the towns on the coaches. Then there were the different accents that emerged with the punters, the excited banter of race day bringing to his ears for the first time the exotic sounds of faraway places like Stoke-on Trent, Dudley and Stafford.

Picture young Jim, earning a few extra bob, taking in the colour and excitement as well as flicking through the papers, spotting the tipsters' naps. More than once the clerk of the course had warned him that 'there'll be no print left on those papers the way you're going on'. The naps went back with him when he collected his Dad's bets to take to the illegal bookies in the back streets.

> Looking back, it was hilarious really because everybody in those days had *noms de plume* on their bets. Then, if the police seized them, they wouldn't know who it was. My father's *nom de plume* was Frank L. They would have had him immediately.

Jim started to have the odd small bet and he was cuter. His *nom de plume* was *Jinx* named after the nag which pulled the baker's van and, one suspects, the only horse seen regularly in those days in Ward End, on the east side of the city.

Jim's Dad was an engine driver for the old London, Midland and Scottish Railways. 'We were working class without being in any way poverty-stricken. The thing about being an engine driver was that the job was secure, the money was good, as long as you worked the hours.'

Even so there was no question of the family finances being good enough to allow Jim to go to grammar school when he passed the exams. At 12 he can remember a set-to between his mother and father as to whether they could afford for him to go to technical college when he also passed those exams. In the end Mother won the day when she would brook no further arguments. 'He's going and that's it.' As Jim says, it lifted him up one step of the long ladder.

When he left at 16 he worked as a junior clerk in an electrical company and at 18 it was time for National Service. 'I signed on for three years; you got more money for the extra year. I was always interested in money.'

Life changed when his mother and father died in their fifties just a short while apart. He found himself as a 19-year-old responsible for a younger brother and sister. Somehow they managed, the local council letting them keep their house and helped by what he describes as 'the best kind of working class community', everybody in the street working to keep the family together.

As soon as he left the RAF, he got a job as a hod carrier – 'It paid good money but I've got the scars to this day.' Then he did a stint on a lathe in a factory making car gears before taking his first proper step along what these days is called a career path. He became a sales rep for a typewriter company, working Birmingham areas 4 and 5 with nothing to help but his feet, the local buses and his cheek and charm. 'It was hard but it was a wonderful background for

a businessman. What you learnt was that only one beggar can make you a success and that's yourself.'

By now ambition was burning in the young salesman's breast – he wanted to be a rep with a car. So in 1957, the year that he and Valerie married, Crosse and Blackwell took him on to sell their range of sauces, baked beans and pickles. Part of the deal was a shiny Morris Minor 1,000, renewed every year but always in black.

'I did well there. I suppose that I suddenly grew up. I thought to myself: "I know how to succeed. You have to work your tatties off." There was a salesman of the year award, a keenly fought contest among the 90 young men who made up the sales force.

Jim saw his chance. Instead of calling on his regular clients – shop owners and café and canteen managers – once a month, he turned up once a fortnight. Jim told the clients

Two men with cause to celebrate - Jim Lewis with Terry Biddlecombe who, with his wife Henrietta Knight, trains Best Mate and Edredon Bleu.

about the contest. The more goods they took, the more points he got. Soon the award was as important to the clients as it was to Jim. When they said they couldn't sell those great big jars of salad cream, he changed their minds by pointing out that the jars carried extra bonus points. Soon all they wanted to talk about was how he was doing in the contest. In the process, says Jim, he was learning all about personal relationships and loyalty. 'You really did learn about those important things. It stood me in good stead later on.'

Of course, being Jim Lewis, he won by a mile and off he and Valerie went on their prize. 'It was five days in Paris in the springtime, all expenses paid. It was our biggest adventure ever.'

By 1961 he was a rep with Slumberland beds and at 33, their youngest ever sales director. Then it was off to Yorkshire where for 14 years he was managing director of the upholstery division of Silent Night beds. It was, he says, a 'bloody good job' with all the perks you could think of. He had a wife, two kids and a mortgage - and eventually a hankering to work for himself before it was too late.

Aged 45, he moved to a 30 acre farm near Evesham and set himself up importing pine furniture from South Africa, selling it in the UK by mail order. 'I called it Spearhead because I saw myself as the spearhead for these guys making furniture in South Africa who didn't have any marketing push until then.'

About five years ago that business was sold to - in effect - his suppliers. 'I'm proud of the fact that business was always run on trust and a handshake. And that's how I sold it. We did alright as they say.'

The other side of his successful home grown enterprises was a business importing agricultural machinery, grass cutters and the like, again from South Africa. Eventually, his daughter Samantha and son-in-law Martin took over Spearhead Agricultural Machinery. He gave them the shares as their wedding present, saying that they could pay him back, if ever, when they could. 'That business now has a turnover in excess of £7 million, all British-made from their factory in Pershore - and every penny of the money I had invested was paid back to me years ago, making me very, very proud.'

Making up their family is son Marvin and at 6 feet 5 inches he towers over his parents. At 33 Marvin has already made a successful start in business, running his own firm importing leather for upholstery and other products. In one respect at least he has his father's full attention. Of his as yet unmarried son he jokes: 'Do you know, he must have had more girlfriends than Richard Burton. Valerie has a wardrobe full of unused wedding hats.'

It was in Jim's twenties, with groups of pals and some money in his pocket, that horses started to play a part. He always went in the cheap end at the Cheltenham Festival. 'You paid £2 to get in to stand on what was really a pile of rubble. We'd have a bet, have a drink and I used to think how great it would be to have a horse, but I knew I couldn't afford it.'

By the mid 1980s, as he rose up the success ladder, there was more money around and the itch to own was still very much there. A half share in a horse called Dawn Fox was the first. 'He'd won 12 chases before we had him but although we had seconds and thirds, he never won for us. I learnt all about trainer speak. 'Didn't like the ground'; 'probably wants further'; 'you can put your mortgage on him next time.'

A horse, Glen-Roy-Boy, advertised by trainer P.J.(Paul) James, was the next. 'I went to look at him and Paul told me the price was £5,000. That I couldn't afford and said if he was ever looking for someone to make up a syndicate with the horse, I would be interested. There and then he dropped the price to £3,000 and I said *yes*.' Sad to report, Glen-Roy-Boy didn't win either, although their son-in-law had great fun riding him in point-to-points.

Jim and Valerie Lewis with one of their three Cheltenham Gold Cups won by Best Mate.

By now, it's 1987, August 10th to be precise - Jim and Valerie Lewis are celebrating their pearl (30th) wedding anniversary with a trip to Doncaster Bloodstock Sales with Paul James. Jim had resolved that if he saw the right horse this would be the day he fulfilled the promise made to his then 14-year-old girlfriend all those years before. But this was to be a surprise present. When he saw what he thought was the right horse, an unnamed three-year-old, he set himself a limit of £10,000.

There I was, sitting in the middle of Valerie and Paul, and suddenly I had to buy him. I kept nodding and finally got him for £12,000. Valerie realised when I signed the note that I'd bought him. I said 'Happy Anniversary' and said we would call him 'Pearl Prospect' and that he would run in her colours, the claret and blue stripes worn by Aston Villa when they won the Cup in 1957.

Paul James had the horse – but when he had proved himself in two decent bumpers Paul – ' We're still mates' - said it would be best if he found another trainer who had the set-up to get the best out of him. And so it was, thanks to a copy of the *Field* chanced upon in a Pershore coffee shop, that Henrietta Knight came into the Lewis lives. 'On the front page of the magazine there was this woman with a dog sitting on a bale of hay. The headline said something like *Queen of Point-to-Point goes NH racing*. I thought well, we could give her a go and I wrote to her and arranged a meeting.'

So it was one of the most successful partnership in modern NH racing got under way. But there was one more element which makes you wonder about all the superstitious stuff that both Jim and Henrietta Knight go in for. The trainer already knew more than a bit about the horse. In fact she was the part-owner of the Kambalda gelding and had prepared him for to the sales.

Sure enough, Pearl Prospect, now trained by H. Knight, was the first winner for the Lewis's - and the rest is history.

Jim says of his relationship with Henrietta and her husband and co-trainer, Terry Biddlecombe:

Our relationship is a bit special. I think they are as fond of us as we are of them. We talk on the phone when it's urgent but we have an arrangement that we do most of it by fax. We have quite a few things in common with Hen. We're both superstitious, and we're both meticulous about what we want. We both have the ability never to have an argument - and we never have. It's all done diplomatically. It is very special.

We put down our points, for and against, on paper. We don't sit on the fence because otherwise you never get anywhere, always saying 'on the other hand.' Hen and Terry have one vote each and Valerie and myself, one vote. We set a day by which we have to decide and we toss it back and forth until that day arrives, Then I put our vote on the fax. Mind you, Terry says that we have a majority decision - but then Hen says what will happen.

But what about the rumoured eccentricity of the trainer and her husband, the fact that some people call them Mrs

Dotty and Mr Potty behind their backs. 'When you get to know them there's nothing odd about them at all. First of all, they are very much in love. It's a great romance. Terry, and to lesser extent, Henrietta, have seen some bloody hard times and it's almost as if they realise they've been given another chance and between them they have created another life. They are a remarkable couple with an incredible sense of humour. They're dedicated to their racehorses, pure romance is what it is.'

Jim is certainly not without his little ways. There's the lucky black cat that gets held aloft when he's leading in his winners; a different lucky tie for each horse; the Best Mate lucky overcoat; the his and hers Aston Villa racing silks; and then there's the humming. It's the one thing that Trainer Knight says she cannot abide. Villa fans have adapted the words of Amazing Grace to their own purpose. By tradition, because it would be unlucky not to, Jim and party hum the adapted version, while his horses run. Perhaps, said somebody, it explains why Henrietta Knight is so reluctant to watch a race. What she's really doing is getting away from the humming.

Superstition is also the reason why Best Mate's Gold Cup victories have been celebrated at the same time in two different venues, one at Best Mate's stable at West Lockinge Farm near Lambourn and the other at Jim's local pub. Once, when Jim was out of the country on business, two of his horses won. Now, because you mustn't push your luck must you, he never goes to the Knight set-up during the season.

As to the other important person in the partnership, jockey Jim Culloty, says Lewis 'We call him the Cool Dude. He looks on Terry as his mentor and they talk racing all the time. Sometimes he's more nervous than others, but usually he's got a marvellous temperament. Not like Hen and me. We get so nervous, it's best if we don't talk to each other before a race because we just set each other off. Jim

Culloty, he'll do for me. He's particularly brilliant at judging pace in a race. He's loyal, he's sensitive - and he cares.'

Wherever it comes from, there's no doubting that there is Lewis luck. And it can even rub off on others. In the race-card owners slot next to Foly Pleasant you will find *Jim Lewis and friends*, the only syndicate he has ever been involved with. And that was against his better judgement.

Some pals nagged him into it. 'When you're on your own there are no complications. You stand or fall on your own judgement.' But the nagging paid off. Including Jim, there are nine in the syndicate, three of them in South Africa who have never seen the horse run.

Jim's worst fears were realised when the horse almost immediately got a leg and had to be fired, writing off season one. But then 'bugger me he turned out to be a very nice horse and we've won some good races with him.' The end result is that since the firing bill no syndicate members has had to pay out a penny. In fact, although the horse hasn't won for two years, there's still £40,000 sitting in the kitty.

You never stop being aware that you are very lucky. I see guys, they've just had their first winner, there could be 30 or 40 of them in the syndicate, they're over the moon. That's what it's all about. It's brilliant.

Of course, you always have to appreciate in jump racing how narrow the gap is between triumph and disaster. There's a terrifying loneliness every time your horse goes out. And of course if that horse is odds – on for the Gold Cup, that's another burden, with all that money thousands of people have risked.

But what about envy, does he ever have to deal with people who resent his success. 'You'd be naïve if you thought that some people don't resent it. I've known since I was a lad that some people just don't like popular people. You have to understand that not everybody is going to think you're God's wotsits.'

But I have never had a problem with any of my fellow owners. At Hen's last open day, when they were parading all the horses in the yard with all their owners there, I was asked to say a few words. I said 'I realise that Best Mate is not the apple of your eye. Your apple is your horse - and that's the way it should be. But you have never resented my success - and for that I want to thank you.

So how did he come by the two horses who between them have brought such glory? It was Henrietta via the legendary Irish horse breeder, Tom Costello, who first saw the potential of Matey and offered him to Jim. The price has remained a secret between Tom and Jim (even Henrietta doesn't know) to this day.

A chance meeting in a Newmarket car park with a Frenchman called Charles Le Metayer eventually led to the purchase of Edredon Bleu. That was relatively straightforward, a £50,000 purchase which can safely be said to have paid off.

Now, as well as the horses already mentioned, there are three youngsters in Tom Costello's hallowed fields who, it's hoped, will carry those now famous Aston Villa silks. Then, at Henrietta Knight's, there are Stars Out Tonight, Blazing Guns, Tuesday's Child, Red Dawn, Chase the Sunset and Jeffertiti.★★

Clearly, Jim Lewis has had his share of luck along the way - but it can't all be luck. He has proved with Valerie ('Hen always says she has a good eye for a horse') to be a shrewd judge - of people, I suspect, as much as of horses.

★★ Sadly even the Lewis luck could not hold forever. Having never lost a horse at the races, the youngster he rated most highly, six-year-old Rosslea, which he believed a Gold Cup prospect, broke a shoulder while racing prominently in a grade A novices' chase over the demanding fences at Punchestown at the end of April and had to be destroyed. It would seem the chances of Best Mate ever running there will have been considerably diminished.

Surely, I put it to him, he at least must have made money at this lark if anybody has?

I'm having a brilliant retirement. You know when I was working I used to describe myself as an apprentice pensioner. I am a lucky boy - and yes we have made money from racing because of the big races we've won. But generally the money we've made we've ploughed back.

What it's done for Val and me is to give us a life we would never have had. Can you imagine taking your two grandchildren into the Royal Box at Cheltenham after you've won a really big race?
Oh how Val and me wish our parents could have seen that.

In life, and I've said this to my son, don't get to sixty and be staring into the embers of a fire and thinking 'I wish I'd done that.' Far better to give it a go, even if you make a cock-up.
I know that one day our seam of gold in racing will run out and some new guy will take over. Do you know, I'll be very happy for him and he can be Lucky the Second.

But I'll know I have been really lucky because I can sit here and say that I've had a really fulfilling life.

Chapter
9

David's Diary 4

DECEMBER 13

Never before in a longish life have I ever known a day on which joy has been quite so rapidly replaced with gloom.

Barely 48 hours after our 'adventures' at Huntingdon where Burwood Breeze had fallen at the last, here we are, all of the Four for Fun team, at Cheltenham, the place which has a special place in the hearts of all jumping enthusiasts. I still get a thrill just going to the place as an ordinary racegoer at what has to be the best jump venue anywhere.

That said, I will continue to mutter about the facilities. Sometimes I blink at the cost of entry considering the difficulties of getting a sandwich, a drink or even going to the toilet in semi-civilised conditions. Whichever member of the management team it was who signed off the work in that gentlemen's toilet in Members should be offered to the hounds next countryside day. The one (yes one) hand-drying machine has been strategically placed at the only entrance and exit door to cause the maximum traffic jam. And then there's that self-service restaurant, again in Members, which has food and comfort standards that bring the memories of 1970s motorway service areas flooding back. Strangely enough the prices don't conjure up the same memories.

But when you turn to the track itself, its setting and the standard and organisation of racing, well … it is an entirely different story. This day sees the main events of the Friday\Saturday Tripleprint meeting, one of the highlights of the Cheltenham year leading up to the March Festival which year in, year out provides racing of such staggering quality and drama. To come as a spectator is terrific - to come as an owner is obviously another thrill again.

Today will see the Tripleprint Gold Cup and the Tote Bula Hurdle. No, we are not involved in either of these - but Jessie MacDougall is to fly our blue and white colours in the first race on the card, the Tripleprint Juvenile Novices' Hurdle Race, a Class B for three-year-olds with £17,500 in prize money and a race which is very much a trial for the young hopefuls who will compete in the Triumph Hurdle at the Festival in just a few months.

There is not a shadow of a doubt in any of her owners' minds that this is way out of Jessie's class, a fact demonstrated by my bet of £5 each way invested on the betting exchanges by partner Terry. The £5 place has been taken at 50/1 but the win bet has been accepted at the rather more exotic odds of 409.08 to 1. Now Terry did explain how that came about and for a moment or two I did understand. Five minutes later I confess I could only see the funny side.

We were, of course, letting her take her chance to complete the three races which would give her an official handicap mark and so proceed to pitch her against rivals in her own league. So we were a relaxed crew - four people who are friends as well as racing fans - who went into the pre-parade saddling area. If our horse came last it was not the end of the world and anything better would be a bonus.

Talking with the Doc we agreed the instructions for jockey Mark Bradburne (selected this time from agent Russ James's list) would be to make sure she finished (to get the handicap) and not to push her too hard. We also agreed that if she beat the only rival in the race remotely in her class we would be well satisfied.

So we were all smiles as she was paraded and in bright sunshine made our way to the Owners' and Trainers' viewing area. Ahead a decent marquee lunch which Cheltenham - following in the pioneering footsteps of Haydock - now provide for owners with runners on the day.

When you think of the owners' costs in terms of buying a horse and keeping him or her in training let alone entry fees, transport and jockey costs, the fact that Huntingdon - where we'd been 48 hours earlier - struggled to run to a free cup of coffee, all you can say is 'thanks' to the tracks that really do make you welcome.

The sun had come out, Cleeve Hill looked magnificent and the horses, ours included, were on their way to post. Overnight rain had turned the official going from good to good to soft. It wouldn't do our cause any harm. More cause for smiles.

The big screen told us that she was being offered at 500\1 - yes 500/1. I don't know when I last saw a horse at quite such a price.

For the first mile Jessie was in mid-division and hurdling well. You want a horse that doesn't so much jump the hurdle as take it in it's stride. The hurdling promise of trainer Evans was being fulfilled.

It was coming down the hill that she seemed to tire and the jockey took a tug conserving her energy and making sure the most important part of the instructions - make sure she finishes to get her hurdling handicap rating - would be fulfilled. To that point it had been a reasonable run but now it looked as if the script would unfold as we had all expected. How far would she finish behind?

But Jessie had other ideas. As she completed the downhill (and she has never looked at her happiest on the downhill part of any track) and took that turn leading to the famous uphill Cheltenham finish she picked up, and although the jockey treated her as we'd asked there was our Jessie picking off rivals. Now there are limits to fairy stories - but can you imagine how we felt when our little home-bred whom we had seen born, our 500/1 shot, had come fifth of the eleven with horses trained by no lesser luminaries than Jonjo O'Neill, Nigel Twiston Davies and two from the Martin Pipe empire behind our girl.

As a result of the race, the top two in the Triumph Hurdle ante post market - and the first and second in this race - swapped places. This was exalted stuff indeed.

The Doc said that all four of us looked both shocked and overjoyed at the same time. Whooping with delight, Terry went off to get photographs of our heroine while the ladies headed with me to the unsaddling enclosure. On the way, what thoughts of what might be to come. Realistically we had always thought that she might make a Class E horse or if we were really lucky, a Class D - in every sense 'a fun horse'. While there were limits to the new dreams, the possibilities were considerably more than they had been just a few minutes before.

As we waited for our horse to arrive someone pointed out there were prizes up to sixth place. We were going to get all of £382 plus £300 appearance money for our fifth spot. Who cared - but there would certainly be enough for the bottles of champagne which would soon accompany our celebration lunch. But where was she? All the other horses were in and the usual huddles around horse and jockey were formed

And then there she was, minus rider and saddle, the clear as daylight signal that there was a problem. 'Is she all right' I immediately asked anxiously of a woebegone young Emily. She was leading the horse whom she'd plaited so beautifully so Jessie looked her very best on the big day. Her face and that of the jockey, trainer and vet told the story.

Jessie had broken down. The initial diagnosis was a rip in a tendon. A year off, box rest for a couple of months followed by firing and then six months in a field. Of course there would always be a concern of it happening again but there it was.

Jockey Mark Bradburne told me that good mares in particular will keep on going with this kind of injury. With the adrenalin pumping in the race, the good ones' battling spirits keeping them going – the kind of racing instinct as an owner you pray for alongside that other prayer to the gods: 'Keep them sound.'

The jockey, clearly upset at what had happened to a little horse who had run so far above expectations, also explained that if he had given her a hard race he was sure we could have got 4th place. The *Racing Post* was to say later that the fourth placed horse had run respectably '... and in the end was not far clear from no-hoper Jessie MacDougall, who was never remotely competitive but stayed on to close on tired rivals who had a lot more use made of them.'

It was all an odd sensation. During the latter stages of the race I kept thinking I was going to wake up from a good dream and then without pause I was in a nightmare which was equally unbelievable. Jessie limped the few strides into the horse ambulance and then was off to the equine centre which is reputedly the best on any UK or Irish track. 'Well' said the Doc 'if you have to have a horse break down this is the best place it can happen.'

And he then cast a glance around Cheltenham in all its glory and said wistfully 'And just when you get a horse that really can run at Cheltenham ...' Dreams are not confined to owners.

Lunch was a somewhat subdued affair, although taken with the sport's aristocracy – Jim Lewis, the amiable owner of Best Mate to our right and the Martin Pipe party to our left. A few drinks helped and I was trying to put the most positive light I could on the afternoon's events. 'Even if we do lose 12 months she'll still only be a five-year-old and we won't even have lost a full season. Remember, we were thinking of one more run after today – and sometimes these things don't take a full 12 months.'

But even that second-best dream was not to be.

By the next day a visit by Terry to see the vet produced the news that it was not just a rip, it was a complete rupture. Her career as a racehorse - short of odds that would make 500\1 look very skinny indeed – was over.

What sort of a future could she have? The prognosis of vet and trainer was pretty grim. We all spent a long night tossing and turning , trying to view the problem from every angle; in honesty trying to find a realistic positive view which would give the horse some reasonable prospect of a decent life.

All our previous horses have been found decent homes once their racing days were over. They have useful lives as hacks, showjumpers or event horses.

For Jessie, the one realistic option was treatment and rest over a four month period and then perhaps a role as a brood mare. But neither couple in Four for Fun have the land needed for that. And who could tell at this stage how sound she would be even after a period of rest? Yes, we could offer her as a brood mare but while she is reasonably bred she is not from a wonderful lineage. Goodness knows where she might finish up in those circumstances.

The next day produced a consensus view. We would ask our former partners, Len and Sue Ballinger, if they would take her. It was on their farm - once described by my daughter as 'horse heaven' - that Jessie had been born and in whose care she had stayed until we amicably dissolved the partnership. If not, the grim fact was the only sensible thing to do was to have her put down. Horrible - but sensibly the only other route we could travel.

In fact our former partners did not hesitate. We would settle the bill for her initial treatment (including special injections to give the natural healing process every chance of success) and then they would own the horse to do with as they chose. Whatever that was, we knew they would put her interests first.

It's a hard game and I know that we were all close to tears more than once in what was a horrible 24 hours. But Jessie, like all racehorses, was bred to do a job. If there was no racing how many thoroughbreds would there be in the world?

Horses race each other and jump obstacles in the wild – and when a horse falls in a race, what's its natural instinct? To get back with the other horses and try to get to the front.

All that said, it was still a time in which some difficult questions had to be faced. To be honest, I don't know how much of it I could take if it happened too often. Breeze's fall and the sight of those green screens and then Jessie's horrible injury will, I hope, be it for a long while.

The little horse was actually named Jessie MacDougall for two reasons. She was part of a line started by a baker and continued by Len and Sue, all their horses having a floury connection. There was On the Breadline, Crusty Lily, Bakers Dozen and many more. MacDougall's flour kept the baker's line in being while at the same time honouring a lady who died at the age of 80 on a visit to our home. She and her 87-year-old husband were our oldest friends in every sense and he was delighted at the thought that his wife's maiden name would live on, not least because Jessie was such an attractive horse.

He always followed her fortunes and had a few quid on her no matter how often he was told that she hadn't a chance in a particular race.

The sense of relief was great all round – not least for me in knowing that telling him the absolute worst was one phone call I wouldn't have to make.

JANUARY 1

Perhaps the time has come to officially change the spelling of this sport. Instead of 'jump racing' in the conventional manner, how about telling the truth and changing it to the more honest 'b.l.o.o.d.y. f.r.u.s.t.r.a.t.i.n.g'. You are allowed to change the adjective to another of your choice and if it happens to be alliterative, so be it.

It was the events at Exeter as the New Year dawned which provoked such thoughts – but before we come to them at least a cheery update on Jessie MacDougall. She is now back at the farm where she was born and has settled down well. Fortunately the swelling on the leg was much less than in many such cases and that makes the prognosis for the future that much better.

We now know that one of the course vets on duty at Cheltenham when she broke down had recommended that she be destroyed immediately, but the view of the senior man prevailed. Let's hope she makes a really good recovery and one day we shall see her progeny at the races.

Meanwhile Gloster Gunner, who is now up to fast canter, will start training proper in the next couple of days with the Doc; and Klondike Charger is reported 'fat and happy' on his winter hols.

Which brings us to Burwood Breeze, fully recovered from his last fence fall at Huntingdon on his most recent outing. We had him entered to run in a 3 mile 'chase at Warwick on New Year's Eve but with lack of rain still causing problems at many tracks it was time for the drought demon to move over and let the frost fairy wave her frozen wand. No doubt the rain god will be pouring down soon.

A 7.30 a.m. inspection at the Warwickshire track (after a night which saw −3C temperatures) lead to a decision to further inspect at 9a.m. and then it was 'off'.

You really do have to have sympathy for the clerk of the course in these circumstances. Trying to anticipate how and when the frost will come off the ground – particularly if grandstands cast a shadow – is no easy task. Safety is paramount and they are not going to be popular with anybody if they wrongly take an optimistic view and then have to cancel when all the horses, jockeys and public are at the course.

On the other hand, trainer Tom had told me it had not been easy to find a suitable race and that we would be in mid-January before another came up. We were therefore a little surprised to get a message to say that actually they had entered him for a race at Exeter on New Year's Day (which they had forgotten to tell us about). Relief overcame irritation and we were a party of six who went to Devon to support Breeze in the Royal Castle Hotel Handicap Steeple Chase, a Class D over just short of three miles. The prize – £4,259 to the winner after the 20% off takes for trainer and jockey.

Apart from the two owners we had horsey daughter and friend and the judge and lawyer wife. We were not without hope, encouraged not least by the *Racing Post*, two of whose oracles made him their pick and summed up the race by saying: 'Not easy to discount any of the runners but the one to beat could be Burwood Breeze who is weighted to gain a belated first success.'

This was a 0-120 contest and Breeze's official rating of 96 meant that with two horses each off 119, our chap would carry just 10 stones 3lb on ground officially soft – but actually ' just the soft side of good' according to jockey Jason Maguire, who had the ride. Young Mr Maguire looked rather white and cold in the parade ring. He is several inches taller than me but had weighed out a little over five stones less than this proud owner. He confirmed that his New Year's Eve had been a sight less colourful than some.

Trainer Tom was seeing to runners at Cheltenham so in his place to do the legging up was his assistant Kerry with whom I get on well. She is the daughter of a former Irish trainer and has more than enough charm and blarney to deal with me – even if it is disguised in the tones of a pukka English girls school.

Before the race itself, a word about Exeter racecourse. I

have been quite a few times before but never on a day as crowded as on this holiday. A normal crowd is about 2,000. This day there must have been at least 4,000. Now let's be clear, big crowds at small tracks are good news - but only if they can cope.

The whole place is sad and shabby and trying to get a cup of tea and a sandwich (having been defeated by the enormous queues in the far from luxurious owners' and trainers') in one of the ordinary bars was a frankly squalid experience. These standards may have been acceptable in the 1930s and 1940s – but if racing is to survive and attract a new audience it will have to do better than Exeter currently manages.

The Times Course Inspector, Alan Lee, had reported a return visit to the track the day before we went and not for nothing had he marked it down from his previous report three years before. A trip up the road by the Exeter management to Newton Abbot or Wincanton would show them what can be done. They could do worse than collect the executives of Taunton and take them along while they are at it.

The real problem this time was actually trying to see our horse run. It is fine to have clearly marked walkways in the stand but a waste of money if a couple of stewards don't make sure that they are kept clear to let people up and down. You would also have thought there was a safety implication.

To get our horse to these races, allowing for three weeks training since his last run, transport, jockey fee and entry fee (and forgetting any contribution to actually buying him or looking after him after the race) had cost wife and self easily £1,000. In return we received six free entries and six racecards as well as a voucher which we exchanged for soup and a roll and coffee. Nice touch and appreciated with regard to the refreshments but the place was crowded to bursting and a new 'room' set aside for people with a runner on the day a corridor-like joke.

Much more important than any of that is to get a reasonable view of your horse as it runs. Surely it is not too much to have a small area in the stand where owners, trainers, connections and stable staff with runners on the day can actually see their race.

As it was at Exeter, we agreed in the parade ring that there was a not a cat's chance of getting into the stand – already clearly full to bursting, walkways and all - and the best we could do was to try and meet up 'near the big screen' as I and a couple of the others nipped off to the bookmakers' ring (surely not too unreasonable a thing to do either).

The betting ring showed that Breeze was the general 9\2 favourite (his eventual starting price) with some 4\1 and 5\1 about. I placed £50 to win at fives, cursing my earlier decision to accept the 7\2 on offer in the Tote Credit Club where I had put £200 'on the nose'.

Time then to reconnect with the rest of the party with the runners at the post. Some chance. I had to watch the race on the big screen with two of our party, having lost contact with the others in the crush, Mrs Byrne explaining later that she had clambered on to a fence to see something of what was happening.

Breeze ran a blinder, jumping beautifully and held up by Jason in the leading group throughout. He moved through to take up the lead at the fourth from home. At the third and second last you would have put the house and both mothers on him - but on the run in he was caught and passed by the gutsy Jaloux D'Estruval, who was giving our fellow over a stone and a half and looked well beaten half a mile out but rallied under Mark Bradbourne close home.

Normally if a horse of ours runs well we are delighted. To finish in the frame, splendid. Second, terrific. But this time we were frankly disappointed. We really did think he was going to break his duck. If you allow for the fact that he was second, a distance clear of the rest when he fell in his last race, this made five successive seconds.

A dejected Jason slipped off his back. Kerry said she didn't know what to say. Again, he had done everything except win. Had we gone too early? Had the ground suited? Was the trip right? Had he stopped when he got to the front? All the usual questions and, to be honest, all the usual answers.

When Tom put in his two' pennorth by phone, we settled on: perhaps we should hold him to the second last before making a move; the ground was fine; Exeter is a stiff track, perhaps two andthree-quarter miles would be better on the tougher courses; and no, he hadn't stopped running when he hit the front.

We soon got over it. After all he had run very well, he is just eight and seems to be improving, and he had returned safe and sound. Oh yes, and we had just won £1,500 as the second prize .

The next day, with Breeze reported to be absolutely fine, the *Racing Post* was encouraging. 'Burwood Breeze has never actually won but he did nothing wrong here and should be placed to open his account on this evidence.' Wounds and balm.

All being well, we shall look for suitable races in a couple of weeks' time. But not, I think, at Exeter.

JANUARY 22

Ambitions change as you get older. The school of hard knocks and the university of life combine to change youthful hopes.

As I have already observed, it is the ambition of many racing fans to witness racing at all of the 59 tracks which currently operate in the U.K. Indeed, considering the threat to many of the smaller tracks posed by a combination of bookmakers, Office of Fair Trading and the desire of many racecourses to 'pile it high and sell it cheap', anybody so inclined is advised to get on with it. All too soon that number could be drastically reduced and the ghosts of virtual racing could rule.

But, as I say, ambitions change with the passing of the years. I have now decided that I will change my plans in this area of human endeavour. A simple desire to enjoy the many-faceted charms and failings of even the 40 tracks where National Hunt racing is staged seems too simple an ambition. No, I am going to go for something which will put me into a different league. And when you have such a start as mine, why not go for something which really sets you apart?

Instead of just enjoying the racing, surely as an owner I need a degree of involvement to make it worthwhile. No, I don't mean having a winner at each of the tracks. That would be (ho, ho, ho) far too easy. As I am allowed to write the rules of this particular contest, would anybody like to pick up the gauntlet and see if they can beat me to be the first owner to have a horse who has run second in a steeplechase at all the U.K. racecourses? And just to make it really interesting, this is a contest which must involve the same horse and the second places have to be the result of consecutive runs.

And just before you accept the challenge, pause and reflect for a moment that this is a contest which for me is already underway. Any challenger will have to accept that my list so far includes Plumpton, Newcastle, Perth, Huntingdon (o.k., o.k., that one was a 'moral' second – but hey, these are my rules) and Exeter. Good start I'd say. But wait, it gets tougher. Never let it be said I don't relish a fight (now, now – as I said these are my rules).

Here it comes – the card that could already be the knockout blow. I had a word with Burwood Breeze and explained that there was a way he could humour the old feller. Would he mind awfully, just for me (and don't tell the missus or the Jockey Club) if despite the obvious attractions of coming first he could – just this sixth time - make sure he came second? 'Well for you, Dave me old sport' says he swallowing the proffered polos 'I'll see what I can do.'

And so it was on this day at Ludlow racecourse, when no one else was looking in the saddling up boxes, he gave me a big wink, touched the side of nose with his hoof and whispered 'A nod's as good as a wink - but remember to stick £500 on the nose to keep em confused.'

Well, when you have a real talking horse you'd be a fool not to listen. And just to make sure nobody got a whiff of the coup, I rejected the 5\2 on offer early, and made sure that it went on at S.P. (which turned out to be 13/8). That'll really throw any special investigators off the scent.

The rest I suspect you can guess. Burwood Breeze magnificently delivered, beaten a length by The Tall Guy in the Ludlow for Conferences Novices' Handicap Chase, a Class E for horses rated 0-105. And do you know, I reckon the Tall Guy's rider, Carl Llewellyn, and trainer Nigel Twiston Davies, still haven't got a clue about my magnificent scam in which they were the unwitting dupes.

They, like everyone else, thought that Breeze really had yet again run his heart out and given his all. Little did they know that this was just notch six on the belt which will one day lead to first spot in the Second Place Stakes. And just remember, as the top man said: 'and the first shall be last; and the second shall be top most.' O.K. so I made the last bit up. But when second place glory beckons, well the tough have to get going – just ask Breeze. Who knows where we will go next, determined to be different. You want horses that win. Huh, everybody wants them. Coming to a racecourse near you - Burwood Breeze THE second.

Alright, enough. Oh that Breeze could talk and perhaps he then could explain. Where did he get these extreme good manners which demand that he says 'after you' so making sure there is always one other horse which must pass the finishing line before him?

Not in truth that you could complain about the manner of the Tall Guy's victory. We were beaten a length fair and square. And fair and square was how the front two horses beat the others, Breeze ten lengths ahead of the third horse. No complaints either about the way Breeze had been ridden by James Davies, as polite, youthful and professional as when he had ridden Klondike Charger earlier in the season. With his five pound claim, we were off eleven stone and he had ridden him exactly as asked, making his move between the last two in the hope of not getting caught virtually on the line as we were in the previous run at Exeter.

He had been my choice after Tom George had explained that stable jockey Jason Maguire would not be available to us because one of Tom's other runners that day at Taunton would require Jason's special charms. Atlastaboy was, Tom explained, 'a lunatic'. Jason was just about the only person who could get on board. Jason's pal, Jimmy MacCarthy, had ridden the horse to victory – but when he got off in the winners' enclosure he had politely thanked Tom for the ride but said 'never again.' For a pro jockey to turn down the chance to ride a proven winner this horse must be quite something.

In fact, jockey and all, the build up to the race had been a bit more complicated than usual. As well as Ludlow on the Thursday we also had an entry at Chepstow the following day in what was in effect a level weights contest. I hadn't much fancied the look of a Paul Nicholls-trained horse which, in a handicap, would have been giving us a stone (the horse, Silver Birch, duly won).

That left Tom with a problem. He doesn't like running two of his horses in the same race for obvious reasons. Curtins Hill had run a good second just a few days before and the trainer was anxious to run him again before the handicapper upped his weight. I shrugged my shoulders and said I fully understood the problem. Then Tom rang back to say that he just couldn't face the prospect of Breeze running second to Curtins so he was sending the horse elsewhere (to Cheltenham, in fact, at the Pillar Chase meeting on the

Saturday where he ran an encouraging second in the novice chase).

So Ludlow it was, a track that takes a bit of getting to but which is worth the effort. Here improvements have been carried out without ruining the 'feel' of the place. If you want to see tweed mixing happily with town, Ludlow is as good as it gets. Mind you, the idiosyncrasies of the place are many - not least the sound of the passing trains and the four (repeat four) road crossings which go over the track and have to be covered with matting during racing.

But the plusses are many - not least cheerful, friendly staff for whom nothing is too much trouble and whose smiles remind you (in case you have forgotten) that this is supposed to be about putting aside the daily cares and having fun.

As to the race itself, the *Racing Post* summary said that Burwood Breeze was always prominent, he was ridden approaching four out, chased the winner two out and stayed on under pressure. The analysis said : 'Burwood Breeze has now been runner - up six times in his 15 starts. He seems genuine enough but has just the one speed and it is costing him dearly.' As the man said - 'tell me about it'.

After this kind of run you again start to question some of the fundamentals. Was the trip right? If we brought him back to say two and three-quarter miles might that leave a bit of a kick? Or should we go the other way and try three miles two or three to see if he had the stamina to outstay the others?

Were we right to hold him as long as we did? What about the kind of track? One of the At the Races commentators said he obviously needed a stiffer track (but then his previous run was at Exeter). And what about the ground? This was good to soft. His best form, to our surprise, had been on good ground at Perth. Then again, how would he do on a really soft surface?

Then there was his jumping. It was certainly one of his

less fluent performances. James reported that in the course of the race he kept changing his legs and certainly at four of the fences he screwed slightly and went left, losing about a couple of precious lengths overall in the race. Ludlow is a right-handed course. Perhaps he would be better left-handed?

All of those questions - and more - went through our heads as we stood, yet again, in the winners' enclosure in second spot. Yet again, Breeze had given his all, as honest a horse as you could wish - but it was still disappointing and frustrating.

Trainer Tom had gone to Taunton to make sure Jason stayed in one piece - so his wife, Sophie was legging up. We heard just before our race that Atlastaboy had won - and when I spoke to Tom on the mobile immediately after the race, I tried to divert him to his win just minutes before.

Tom was having none of it. He asked us to try and find the handicapper and plead our case on the grounds that we had started our current run of seconds off an official mark of 90 and we were now off 98. I have to say I didn't think the handicapper had been that unreasonable considering the performance of some of the horses we had beaten or had beaten us. Our problem was that the horse was running up to his handicap mark.

But Tom, who cannot abide with a passion coming second ('Well, I shouldn't be doing the job if I did') was insistent. So Sophie and self duly tramped off to the weighing room where the board told us that there was no handicapper present that day.

Tom subsequently had a word with the senior handicapper - and the good news (and good for Tom) was that he wouldn't be dropping us, nor putting us up either. In the end, we decided it was all just one of those things and perhaps Ludlow might be one of my favourite tracks but not, we suspect, his. Meanwhile, Breeze's *Racing Post* rating went back up to 110, equalling his top mark for his second at Perth in the last run of the previous season.

On our return from the weighing room we were invited for a drink in the Ludlow Racing Club bar by another of Tom's owners. As I enjoyed the consoling effects of a large scotch and the discovery that we were £1,159 richer for second place, Sophie and the owner fell into a discussion about a device whose calming effect on plants has been nothing short of miraculous. Now it was being marketed as a possible aid to over-excitable horses. Of one such our host was a part owner, being trained by the Georges at Slad.

The device was produced, literature proffered and studied. I think that I understood about one-hundreth of what was being said. The device, it was explained, would be strapped over the horse's heart and calmness would result.

I had two thoughts. One, would Jason like to give it the ultimate test on Atlastaboy; and two, might it be useful for use on owners during races, particularly those whose horses keep coming second? And surely there should be a special discount for people whose runners have now been the beaten favourite three times on the trot?

FEBRUARY 7

So there we were: me, Mrs Byrne and 22 others in the Persian War private box on a bright, breezy day at Chepstow. With a few exceptions, most of our party were rare visitors to the races and rarer still in the company of horses. But a party we most certainly were.

We were celebrating - just a few days in advance - Mrs Byrne's 60th birthday and friends and family had travelled from far and wide. In the morning, I had donned striped apron to serve up bacon sandwiches, our racing partner had offered guidance with Terry's tips and then it was off to the races.

Sounds simple enough. In fact there had been five days of tension before we got there. As I predicted in the diary for January 1, when drought and the frost fairy were in the ascendant, 'no doubt the rain god will be pouring down soon.' Oh that some of my other predictions were so accurate, especially those involving handing over cash to bookmakers.

The plan had been for some time to get Burwood Breeze to run at the Chepstow meeting as the centre-piece of the racing part of the birthday celebrations. Trainer Tom was happy - and we duly entered him for a three-and-a-quarter mile handicap chase. On the Monday, at the five-day entry stage, we had a word with Tim Long, the very helpful clerk of the course at Chepstow. 'Soft ,heavy places' was the way things stood then - and pressed by us, on the basis of predicted rainfall, that was the way he expected it to be five days later. Not ideal for Breeze but not impossible.

And he was not the only one in our frame. Hearing of our plans for Mrs B's birthday and encouraged by Terry, the Doc suggested that Gloster Gunner could run on the same day in the two mile novices race in what would be his debut over hurdles. Philip and his team were delighted at the progress Gunner had made physically and mentally in the past year - and even more pleased after they schooled him over obstacles.

Of course, what happens at home and at the racecourse can be two, very different, matters. The Doc said ideally he would have given the horse another couple of weeks but the experience would do him no harm and Gunner would give another string to our party bow.

As the week progressed and the rain kept falling, blown into everyone's faces by howling gales, we watched the skies and muttered dark imprecations to the weather gods. On Thursday, the thrice-daily checks on Ceefax updates of the predicted going, suddenly showed Chepstow updated to 'heavy.'

We had made the races a central part of our celebration. There would be supper for 26 in the evening-but hotels had been booked and beds arranged to allow the people from afar to arrive on the Friday evening. How would we keep them entertained until the evening if the meeting was abandoned?

A conversation later that day with Tom revealed a trainer concerned about Breeze and the possible effect of a really hard race in boggy conditions. The horse, he said, was not only honest, always giving of his best, but also not stupid. Another run which left him as exhausted as he was after the seasonal debut at Huntingdon would not be a good idea. For horses, like all athletes, the mental is as important as the physical.

For obvious reasons, I was more than keen to give my wife – and partner of 35 years – the very best birthday possible. How about we review the situation the following morning, the Friday just before the 10 a.m. deadline for declarations?

A twitchy night, with me more than once sticking my nose out of the bedroom window, had me out on our sodden lawn in the driving rain soon after 6.30 a.m. I knew that the case against Breeze running was unanswerable – but would the meeting go ahead with Gunner at least giving a central focus to that part of the day?

Ceefax told us that an inspection would take place at 2.30 p.m. to determine whether racing could go ahead the next day. At 3.30 p.m., with no televised update, I rang the course. Any news? 'Not yet' was the answer. Why so long? 'Because they are checking every part of the course' was the next answer.

Soon after 4 p.m. we were still in business – just. They would inspect again at 7.30 a.m. the next morning. Another, even more, twitchy night. But in the nick of time, the threats, curses and prayers were answered. The night was dry and the morning bright and cold. Racing would go ahead.

Sorting a jockey for Gunner had not been easy. Of the three meetings that Saturday only Sandown was certain. Wetherby, like Chepstow, was subject to an early morning inspection. It meant that for many horses and jockeys, plans could only tentative.

We needed to be sure that whoever took the ride clearly understood that our horse had to be handled sensibly. This was his first crack over hurdles and only his second–ever visit to the races. What we didn't need was a pilot who might have a sudden rush of blood to the head.

From the start the Doc suggested Jody Mogford, who's ridden quite a few horses for the stable in recent times. With the Doc in surgery, I took on the jockey allocation. Injury and prior calls meant that several of the people we had used and we knew would ride as we asked, were unavailable. When I spoke to jockey agents, Dave Roberts and Russ James, to ask who they had free I got an appreciative response when I said that I could imagine what fun they were having with two thirds of the next day's jump racing uncertain.

In the end we settled on the Doc's choice - and Jody got the ride. We'd drawn lots to decide who from our party, would go into the middle at parade time. Terry went into the middle plus Mrs Byrne accompanied by eight ladies in our party (Mrs B. was in charge of the draw).

Our group, plus Teresa Pritchard - in charge with the Doc at Sandown - plus mother Margot and with Emily leading round, meant that Gunner was not short of female attention.

Terry and self had made it clear to everyone that whatever the horse might be in the future, today he was not a betting proposition. My bet was a deeply sensible £10 each way at 50/1. On that score at least we were dead right. Round he went, pulling hard on the first circuit, but clearly enjoying himself and taking seven of the eight hurdles in some style. Only the first caused him to jink, his leap there owing more to a bunny hop than Istabraq.

On the second circuit he started to tire which in the ground was understandable. Considering some of his fellow competitors were on their fifth and six trips to the races, that was unsurprising. He finished tailed off, last of the 13 finishers, but two had pulled up and he had completed. Jody was straightforward when he slipped out of the saddle. 'Nice horse, hated the ground. I'd think next time you should be looking at two and a half miles – and on the soft side of good.'

At Chepstow they unsaddle on the track just past the finishing post. In the sunshine and with a dry wind blowing, Jody headed for the weighing room as Teresa said 'look at this', pointing at the ground. The Irish make a sensible distinction in soft and heavy conditions. They describe the ground as 'holding' or 'yielding'. With the latter, horses will usually go though what is sloppy mud. With the former, the characteristics of the glue pot apply. That day you could see the deep impressions the hooves were making and how much energy the animals must have been using to get their hooves out.

Interesting to note that in the last race of the day, of the 16 starters only four finished, the other 12 all pulling up. Definitely not for Breeze over three and a quarter miles. Tom had been dead right.

As it was Gunner was fine after his run and we have an eye on another outing for him at the end of the month. His education about racing – and ours about him – is progressing.

Our party headed home for the next part of the celebration. By the evening, the ladies had left their racing gear far behind as glamour became the order of the day at a four-course meal. The men were in dinner jackets – my wife's way of making sure that I didn't turn up in one of the sleeveless jumpers of which I am as so fond and she is not.

Before the dancing and the songs, there were choruses of 'Happy Birthday' and speeches – as well as something just a bit different. Mrs Byrne is also a writer. I had persuaded her to let me read (she would have been far too modest) her entry for a *Racing Post* short story competition. Entries had to be less than two thousand words and on a racing theme.

When I first read it through, it made me both laugh and cry. When the party guests heard it, several – including partner Terry – said it had the same effect on them.

See what you think.

Chapter 10

The Connections of Billy Boy

It wasn't just the daily delivery of the *Racing Post* that set Mrs Mountjoy apart from the other 20 residents. Other things – like installing satellite television in her room and tuning it permanently to 'At the Races' – made everyone aware Mrs Mountjoy was ... well she was different. And it wasn't even as if she ever seemed to bet on horses. All enquiries about possible tips were met with:

'No bloody idea.'

But then she would tap the side of her nose and add, mysteriously:

'But I might have ... one day.'

She had been in the home for five years, the longest of any of them and all they knew was she was a widow with no family and that she and her husband had been some kind of farmers.

They were used to her 'colourful' language and because of her seniority and the daily source of interest she provided, they rarely took offence when she chided them for 'sitting about' and 'giving in'.

'Get off your backsides. You'll only get piles or you'll die in the chair and nobody'll notice for a week.'

She was no mean mover herself. She negotiated her zimmer frame around the house as if she was driving a lorry.

'Move over, big one coming through' she would shout as she overtook wheelchairs, walking sticks and other zimmers in the rush for the best seat at lunch. She rarely let the pain she was suffering in her knees show on her face but on damp, cold days it was necessary to ignore her cursing.

'Sod off pain.'

The staff accepted she was 'a character' and bit their lips when she welcomed newcomers at the door with the cheery call:

'Come in, come into the waiting room. We're waiting to die unless you know an alternative.'

But the home was not a depressing, lonely place, Mrs Mountjoy saw to that. Bones ached, breath was short, relatives died and friends got too ill to visit –but she kept up morale with a personality as forceful as her voice.

Little Miss Atkins said she was 'very scary' and Mr Brownlow said she was like a 'runaway tank'. Certainly with her thinning white hair sticking out like a cartoon character who's had a fright, her blue eyes flashing and her teeth rattling (they were a little loose) she was hard to ignore. And she could spot a damp eye from across a room.

'For God's sake Mavis cheer up. You'll frighten the staff. They'll blame themselves and we'll be forced into one of those damned bingo games to cheer us up. We may all have lived too bloody long but we're not handing in the reins yet.

Right, I'll take on all-comers for dominoes – penny a spot. I'd rather live wild than die rich.'

They admired her strength, they loved the way she wouldn't 'give in' and they relied on her to provide flashes of colour in a greying world.

But Mrs Mountjoy knew herself to be a fraud. She had something they didn't. A secret, a purpose for going on and one day she would need them to witness her triumph – she had nobody else. Well, almost nobody else.

Mrs Mountjoy had a 'gentleman caller' and the whole house tried to be around for the twice-yearly visits of Mr Docherty. He was a scruffy little man with a wizened face and a nose like an aubergine. He wore a battered tweed cap and there was also a pungent whiff about him that reminded them of a raw and untamed world outside their centrally heated, balanced diet, controlled environment.

'How are yers all?' he'd call out as he headed up the stairs with a bottle of whisky protruding from his battered tweed jacket. 'Not misbehavin' I hope now.'

During the meeting a number of people found it necessary to walk past Mrs Mountjoy's door and even to pause a little to get back their breath. Through the door they would hear her strident tones deliver some interesting snippets of conversation.

'But what about his arse Pat? Is it big enough?' was one that caused a deal of speculation.

'I'd give my pension to run a hand along those flanks before blowing up his nose' was another.

After a clink of glasses Mr Docherty would leave, tipping his cap to them all.

'God bless yers. Mind yers good till the next time.'

Mrs Mountjoy never referred to the visits and it would have been impolite to pry. Besides there was another 'Mrs Mountjoy event' that caused even more excitement.

Every year on January the 1st they were invited to join her for champagne – four bottles - when she would ask them to raise their glasses to 'wish my Billy Boy a very happy birthday'.

Their reply was heartfelt.

'To Billy Boy. God Bless him.'

Nobody knew who they were toasting or how many birthdays, but they loved the occasion. Mr Carlisle and Mrs Graham giggled and forgot they didn't get on. Mrs Carmichael waved her stick and told slightly risqué stories about Paris in the forties. Mr Thomas and Mr Roberts topped up the glasses while Mrs Thompson, Mrs Morgan and Miss Grey parked their walking sticks next to the piano and sang old songs.

Mrs Mountjoy, her face flushed, would heckle.

'Don't you know anything dirty? Don't think Beverley sisters, think Eartha or that Madonna woman.'

This was the highpoint of her year. She retired to bed with a slight headache and a happy heart. Another year closer. She only hoped she could last out.

Then came Billy Boy's sixth birthday and Mr Docherty said 'yes!' Mrs Mountjoy distributed hand written invitations.

'I would appreciate the company of my friends at the 'coming out' of Billy Boy at Chepstow Races on February 7. Outdoor shoes and warm clothes essential. £20 towards expenses appreciated.'

A race meeting. How exciting. How Mrs Mountjoy. The house was agog. They would meet Billy Boy at last.

It took a special bus, four carers and a lot of patience to transport 21 sets of creaking bones, two wheelchairs, four zimmers, an assortment of sticks and a pair of crutches to Chepstow. But it was a jolly journey through the Cotswolds and across the huge span of the Severn Bridge into the beautiful Wye valley. Elastic stockings, wheezy chests and painful joints were forgotten after a few tots of whisky, some smoked salmon sandwiches and a good old sing-song led by Mrs Mountjoy.

'She'll be wearing pink pyjamas when she comes …'

Mrs Mountjoy herself was somewhat colourfully dressed. Over a bright green suit she'd draped a vivid fuschia shawl and on her head was a green hat with a pink feather that bobbed as she sang.

But the singing hid the fear in her heart. What if she was wrong? What if Pat had simply humoured her? What if the dream could never be? What if her promise to Jock that she'd see Billy Boy got his chance was a waste of time? She couldn't bear the thought.

Anyway it was wonderful to be going to the races again with hope in your heart and a spring in your step – bugger the zimmer. Soon she'd feel wind from the Welsh mountains in her face and the soft turf under her feet (going good to soft … perfect). She would hear the lilting accents and see the ruddy country faces mixed in with the city slicker smiles. There'd be men in trilbies, girls in silly shoes, farmers with an eye for a good horse, young men with an eye for a filly.

Once again she'd see the stable lads and lasses oiling the hooves, checking the boots, rubbing a twitching nose and whispering into revolving ears:

'Go for it – and come back safe.'

Jockeys in their rainbow colours would salute the owners while trainers issued their instructions.

'Keep him well up. He's genuine. He'll give what he's got, but mind the water – spooks him.

Where else could you talk so easily to a stranger?

What do'ye fancy in the next?'

Where else would £2 buy the thrill of yelling home half a ton of muscled flesh with a proud head, valiant heart and eyes to stop a train?

She longed to walk the course, check the stirrups and set a smart pace around the pre-parade. Instead she and her companions made a slow, shuffling progress across the turf to the centre of the parade ring. With a curious Chepstow crowd looking on they all gathered – the connections of Billy Boy.

'Here he comes' roared Mrs Mountjoy. 'My beautiful Billy Boy.'

And then as Mr Docherty led in a beautiful horse that towered above him, they understood. Billy Boy was a truly magnificent dark bay with a movement that turned heads and lifted hearts. He ignored the crowd, his flesh gleamed, his muscles rippled and he danced a little on his toes.

'Oh Billy you're beautiful' thought Mrs Mountjoy as she remembered the cold February morning when the old mare seemed reluctant to foal. She had put a bucket of water into the stable and then hobbled back across the yard on her dodgy knees to get a slice of hay.

Jock, looking grey and drawn, had been sitting on a bale.

'She'd better get on with it, or I'll be dead before she has the bloody thing' he grumbled as they helped each other across to the stable. And then a miracle. The old mare, always keen on privacy, had dropped a colt. But not just any colt. A colt they had dreamt of breeding for thirty years. You couldn't put your finger on it, but they knew. This was the one.

Jock and she helped him to his feet and encouraged him to start him suckling.

'Call him after our lad. Call him Billy. Give him every chance. He'll not let you down' Jock had said with tears in his eyes.

Such joy followed by such sorrow. Jock joined their son in the graveyard. The farm was sold up. She booked her place in the home and Billy Boy went off to Ireland. She hadn't seen him since.

And now a man with a microphone was approaching. His tone was the teensiest bit patronising to Mrs Mountjoy's ear.

'How nice to see you back after all these years – it must be 10 since you had a runner.'

'Eight years, three months and two days' she replied.

'And you've brought this horse over from Ireland. No real form – what do you reckon his chances?'

'My Billy Boy would run the bollocks off the lot of them – if they had any' she boomed. The crowd roared and the connections nodded smugly.

'Atta girl' called Mr Roberts. 'Well said' quipped little Miss Grey.

The jockey, in colours of green and pink touched his cap before climbing on board to Mrs Mountjoy's call: 'Look after him – we've plans'.

And so it was that Billy Boy stayed mid division for the first mile clearing eight fences in style. At the sixteenth he made a mistake but held onto his jockey to take the next five in third place. At the 22nd the connections gasped as he stretched out his front legs and the power from his rear drove him into second.

They whispered: 'Go on Billy Boy!' 'And then their

cheer was young and strong as he cleared the 23rd to beat the competition up the Chepstow Hill. 'Yes!'

The presentation was delayed to allow the connections to make it into the winners' enclosure but not before Mrs Mountjoy ran a knowing hand along Billy Boy's sweating flanks. She blew up his nose. 'Thank you Billy Boy, thank you … you and your beautiful big arse.'

There was a cup for the winner plus £3,000. Mr Docherty got a giant bottle of Irish whiskey and the connections discovered that their 'contribution towards expenses' had been put 'on the nose' at 25 to 1.

Mrs Mountjoy truly was a dark horse.

Chapter
11

David's Diary

FEBRUARY 12

O.K. The facts. Straight. Unspun. Without embellishment. But one word of warning. Just be careful you don't get splashed by the tears.

The course - Huntingdon. The race — the Tote Bookmakers Novices' Handicap Chase, a Class C, 0–125, over three miles with total prize money of around £13,000. Of that, the jockey and trainer will share £2,118 and the winning owner, £6,315.

Fourteen horses are due to go to post, Burwood Breeze being one of them, carrying ten stones seven pounds. In the saddle, a jockey whose name may ring a bell, A.P. McCoy. This, of course, the chap who had but recently crossed the 2,000th winner mark, making him by far and away the most prolific winning jockey that National Hunt racing has ever seen. Some say one of the best, and many would say THE best.

You would have to be an odd sort of owner not to want this man in the saddle, particularly as the last six runs with Breeze have involved five seconds. The odd one out, as you may recall, being our previous outing to Huntingdon and the last fence fall when a distance clear of the others, in - of course - second place.

There were a couple of oddities about another horse in the race, Bacardi Boy. First, he is part owned by Mr Terry Warner, whose Rooster Booster won the 2003 Champion Hurdle. I had never met Mr Warner in the flesh but had spoken to him by phone only a couple of days before the race to fix the interview which resulted in Chapter 6 of this book.

We knew that we both had horses entered but thought it unlikely we would meet because his horse is best headed towards heavy while ours (we think) is inclined towards good. But with it officially 'soft, good to soft in places' but unofficially drying out, we were both there.

The other odd fact is that when we bought Breeze, we had a choice of three horses, one of the other two being Bacardi Boy. Now whether it is wise to turn down animals chosen by owners whose horses have won Champion Hurdles is for others to decide. What can't be disputed is the fact that Bacardi Boy has won several races. I had watched his progress from afar, wondering inevitably if I had made the right choice.

Terry and his wife, Jill, plus trainer Tom and our foursome – self, Mrs Byrne (celebrating her actual birthday), her racing-mad cousin and our horsey daughter – all chatted happily together in the parade ring. The *Racing Post* had said of our chances: 'Seems genuine enough but lack of finishing pace responsible for his severe bout of seconditis in staying handicap chases. Every chance from a handicapping viewpoint with no ground worries and the booking of Tony McCoy could finally work the oracle.'

Certainly the punters seemed to agree, making him 3/1 clear favourite at the off. I had thought long and hard about my bet this time. His last six efforts, commendable in terms of jumping, effort and consistency though they had been, had made me popular with the bookies but not in quite the same category with my bank manager.

But having been through the race in some detail I did think that at the weights, he had an excellent chance. So I had filled in the Tote Credit Club voucher for £400 on the nose and laid another £20 as a reverse exacta on trainer Tom's alliterative pair, Bacardi Boy and Burwood Breeze.

In the ring, it was jockey Jason Maguire who had been claimed to ride Bacardi Boy who first came into view. He gave me a smile and wished us good luck – and I did the same in reverse. And then there he was, Tony McCoy, the jockey whose skills and determination have made him that rare being, a legend outside his own sport.

Up close you could not say he exudes a ruddy-faced health. In fact the white bits in our colours were well matched. When we talked about the upcoming race it was clear the champion was well briefed. He had taken on board the bit about not getting to the front too soon and to try and keep him with a horse in front until between the last two fences.

He told us that he didn't know how many winners his tally stood at that moment – but it was not enough.** And to rest assured, the only person who wanted to win this race more than us was one Tony McCoy. And then, after my usual invocation to come back safe, which was returned with what seemed a very sincere 'thank you', he was in the saddle and on his way, customary stone-face in place.

In the race itself, Breeze travelled well throughout, his jumping back together without the little screws we had seen at some of the fences at Ludlow. Interesting to watch a master craftsman getting to know a horse he had only seen for the first time a few minutes before. The jumping got better and better, as champion and horse grew in confidence together, becoming ever bolder as the race went on. In fact, that just might have been our undoing – but in a way nobody could have predicted.

At the top turn, about a mile from home, the leader stole about six lengths. Breeze had been in the leading half dozen throughout and was asked by McCoy to quicken to make

---

** He eventually finished with 209 winners from 800 rides. And having become champion jockey for the 8th time he surprised everyone by announcing he was leaving Martin Pipe to join Jonjo O'Neill.

up the gap. He responded and with Bacardi Boy alongside the two pals from the training gallops were bowling along. At the fourth last, Breeze was asked for a big one and more than delivered, taking three or four lengths out of the others. Absolutely terrific. This really looked like being our day at last.

But there was a problem in the shape of the horse who had stolen the lead. He had run his race and was rapidly backtracking. So between the fourth and third last fences we were where we didn't want to be - several lengths in the lead.

And then it happened. About three lengths from the fence with no warning, Breeze did a right angle turn and ran out, unshipping the champion in the process. Breeze ran round the fence and then quite happily rejoined the race, leaving the champion to make his own way home on foot - nothing, apart from his dignity, dented.

Meanwhile, in the race itself, Bacardi Boy was as puzzled as the rest of us as to what had happened to his friend. One minute there they both were and the next he was on his ownsome. He finished fifth, meaning that thoughts of a Tom George 1-2 had more than shrivelled.

In the unsaddling enclosure, a perfectly happy Breeze, who had been neatly caught by stable-hand Alice, was not joined by his rider. In fairness McCoy had a ride in the next. So we sent Tom to ask the obvious 'what happened?' To his credit, the jockey did say that it would have been better if he had his whip in the other hand but then Breeze had given no warning and had never done anything remotely like this at the racecourse before.

But in truth, when younger, he had become notorious for suddenly whipping round and unseating his jockey on the training gallops. He had just about everyone off - Tom and Jason included - before it was decided that wherever else he went in the string it was not going to be out front.

Quite what we do now leaves room for speculation. Some years before when I was a TV producer I had seen the trick that's used by Lloyds TSB Bank to get those wonderful pictures of the black stallion for their Black Horse logo sequences. You know the one - where the splendid animal crashes through the surf, every inch magnificent, as it gallops straight and true.

The trick - position your cameras carefully. Timing in this is all. Then introduce a mare in season on the other side of the bay. Get the cameras turning and yourself out of the way and hey presto you have the black stallion in very full flight.

Of course Breeze is a gelding so the Black Horse approach won't quite work in all aspects. But do you suppose we could persuade the stewards to let us have another horse amble past the winning post just as the runners come into view for the final time? That way he'd still have another horse to aim for.

Of Breeze's performance the *Racing Post* said: 'A modest handicap chase that was run at a reasonable pace but the form has to be questioned as the favourite Burwood Breeze was seemingly going the best when he swerved and unseated his rider approaching three out.

Burwood Breeze was in the process of running a big race until he got rid of his rider. He has a bit to prove now but is clearly on good terms at present and is worth another chance in a similar event.'

I'm thinking of presenting my bank manager with a framed copy.

In truth, it seemed a long way back to the West Country that evening. Eventually you do have to see the funny side. But I still think it was a bit mean for somebody to arrange to have Friday the thirteenth a day early - and on Mrs Byrne's birthday too.

And on that one I think A.P. McCoy might agree. Surely nobody could expect him to remember all the thousands of horses he's ridden over the years. But you know, I can't help thinking that even when some of the winners have faded, the memory of Burwood Breeze will linger on.

FEBRUARY 21

And the first shall be last … and the second shall be constant … and the third will make a change.

To be truthful, the events leading up to Burwood Breeze's appearance at Ascot on this Saturday were possibly more interesting than the race itself.

When Breeze decided to depart the race and decant Tony McCoy three fences from home at Huntingdon it seemed that he had not over-exerted himself. He was fit and well and full of it. Knowing that there were two suitable races coming in the following week – one at Sandown on the Friday and another at Ascot on the Saturday – it seemed obviously sensible to get him back to the track as soon as possible.

Trainer Tom George it was who had first suggested the Ascot and Sandown races. By the time we had the five-day entries for both races, the trainer had departed for France for a well-earned half term holiday with his wife and two young sons. I'd looked at the runners for both races and reached the conclusion that I would rather go to Ascot because I thought the Class E handicap there offered an easier race than the Class D novices' handicap at Sandown. I also had my brother over for the weekend from his home in Italy plus a friend to whom I could usefully repay some hospitality. They could do the Saturday but not the Friday. So there were two reasons why Ascot appealed.

Tom rang not long before 'make your mind up' time – 10 a.m. on the Thursday. I made the case for my preference and he for his. In the end something had to give so I said just this once, I would have my way and so Ascot it was.

Was it my turn for stable jockey, Jason Maguire, I asked? Tom replied he would come back to me on that one. What I didn't know at the time and didn't know until just a few minutes before the start of the Saturday race, was that I had played a part in ruining a neat plan Tom had worked out.

He wanted us to go Sandown with Jason on board,

another horse trained by him, Curtins Hill, would go to Wincanton on the Saturday - leaving a third George horse, Redskin Raider, as his sole representative in the Ascot contest. Ah, the best laid plans.

Not only did I not want to go to Sandown, the owners of Curtins Hill didn't fancy Wincanton and wanted to go to Sandown. And that's where Curtins Hill went where he ran out an impressive winner with Jason on board.

That left the stable with two runners in the Amlin Handicap Chase - ours and Redskin Raider. I confess to being a bit miffed on Friday when I was told that Jason would be riding the other horse. I was particularly keen to have him on our horse because he had schooled our chap since he was broken and was best versed in his little ways which had been seen to such effect when the champion jockey got dumped.

Now with just a single horse in the yard - although having been pretty loyal owners over the years - Mrs Byrne and self are not unwise to the facts of life in all this. Where there is a conflict you have to accept that multiple owners have the biggest pull.

I had imagined that Jason would have the choice (just as I had said he could choose earlier in the season). When I was told that he would be on Redskin Raider I couldn't quite believe it. No disrespect to the animal but included in his last four outings were a pulled up, an unseated and a fall. At least we could offer five 2's in our last seven.

I took over the jockey decisions and after speaking to the main agents settled on James Davies, the conditional who had ridden both Breeze and Klondike Charger for us in recent months, including Breeze's second at Ludlow in January.

Such has been James's season that he can now claim only three pounds as he battles it out with Sam Thomas and Jamie Moore for the jump apprentices' title. He had shown us real skill as well as an ability and discipline to ride to orders.★★ With his claim, Breeze would carry ten stones eleven pounds in what would finish up as an eight horse race.

To be honest I was still a little bit sore about the jockey business as Mrs Byrne and self were fixing our badges having just gone through the owners' and trainers' entrance at Ascot. Who should be the first person to say hello, his jockey bag over his shoulder, than Jason Maguire.

He has an easygoing Irish charm which I am sure he has used to good effect both at racetracks and elsewhere. It transpired that he thought we hadn't wanted him to ride our horse and he didn't demur when I said that either he was mad – or I was mad – if he really thought that Redskin Raider had a better chance than Burwood Breeze in this particular contest. He then explained the importance of the syndicate which owns Redskin Raider to the yard – and as, I hope, a grown up I then understood. Jockey and owner parted on friendly terms.

There wasn't time for much of a conversation in the pre-saddling area because with two horses to get ready the George team were fairly stretched and there was just time for Tom to ruefully explain his master plan which he thought would have kept everyone happy.

Ascot like so many courses is something of a building site at the moment – but that said I think it has a special atmosphere even though I have never seen it in full royal fig in the smart and sunny days of June. Horses matter hereabouts – and where else these days do you see that many men in bowler hats outside the Orange Lodge marches in Northern Ireland.

Just before the off, Breeze was a pretty universal 4/1 (his starting price). I had laid £100 off course as a precaution earlier - but when I found the TV bookie, Big Barry 'Bismarck' Dennis in the betting ring offering our horse at

★★ The conditionals championship was eventually won by Jamie Moore.

9/2, I laid £200 at that price. He didn't flinch and neither did the price on his board.

The *Racing Post* had said Breeze had 'obvious claims but was only for the brave'. The writer of the racecard was seriously sticking his neck out. We had, he wrote 'place claims again.'

In the race itself, on this right-handed track, again Breeze showed a tendency to jump left, although not as pronounced as it had been at Ludlow. They had gone off at a fair pace and although James never let him lose touch he was closer to the back than the front for the first couple of miles. He had moved to third place a half mile from home and James was to say later that he felt they had a real chance but he made no serious impression and we finished in third.

Once off his back in the winners' enclosure James, who had again given the horse an excellent ride, said he was a bit concerned there might be a minor problem with his back. The overall verdict from jockey, trainer and owner was that Breeze hadn't shown the same spark as he had in his recent races. Overall it was a below-par performance and perhaps we had under-estimated what the run at Huntingdon had taken out of him.

We had raced him again too quickly, just 9 days after his previous effort. We agreed to have his back checked and to give him a decent break – three to four weeks. And next time, I said as a parting word to Tom, perhaps Jason could be on board?

It was interesting to note that the first two were the two bottom weights, the winner beating us just under ten lengths. The *Racing Post* noted that 'Burwood Breeze … was notably buried on the inside with plenty of horses on his left. This maiden edged closer and did little wrong but ran around under strong pressure in the straight and made a mistake at the last. He may need softer ground.'

To my eye, the mistake at the last was very minor and as for the ground, well he does seem capable of handling anything outside firm and heavy.

Reflecting later, I decided what strange creatures we are (the humans not the horses). I felt better because we hadn't had the trauma, of getting beaten a length, or falling at the last, or running out when in the lead. It was a straightforward third place, with prize money of £676.

And that 3 will at least break up all those 2's.

MARCH 6

It's not, said the man, the winning – but the taking part that counts. Amen to that. And as this diary has shown, the winning has certainly not been easy but now it seems the taking part is getting tougher too.

As already reported, Burwood Breeze is having a mini-break to freshen him before we try and get him to break his duck. Klondike Charger came off his holidays at the beginning of this month and will spend around six weeks doing the basic preparation which will take him from walk up to canter before he heads off for full training. And the news about Jessie MacDougall is as good as we could hope. The vets are delighted with her progress, the tendon has knitted really well and after a period of box rest she is now being allowed out of her stable for a few minutes each day. She is walking normally and is in good health.

Which brings us to the most popular boy in the school, Gloster Gunner. Our five-year-old home-bred is popular with all the stable staff and he has been working hard and, according to the Doc, showing steady improvement in everything he does. All of which is good news – but there is a simple reason why many owners avoid this process and buy ready-made animals off the flat or in sellers. Simply, it all takes a very long time and requires patience all round.

The fact is that we are spending quite a few thousands of pounds on his education and it won't be until he is seven or even eight that we will know whether we have really got a three miles 'chaser which is what his breeding suggests he will make.

There has been a continuing debate between the Doc, Terry and self about the rate of progress and whether or not it is sensible to acknowledge that he will never make a hurdler and crack on with him over 'chase fences.

For the moment at least we are sticking to hurdling, and while I accept that two miles is far too short for him I have resisted suggestions that we should try him over the smaller obstacles but over three miles. I fully understand the fact that the basic speed over three miles will be much slower than over two but have made the point that we should go one step at a time. So for the moment at least, we shall look for opportunities at around two and a half miles.

To that end he was entered to run over that distance at Huntingdon on February 26 in a pretty fancy Class B. We were one of eleven still in at the 24 hour declaration stage. Not surprisingly he was the rank outsider. That wasn't a problem - the trouble was the weather. The frost fairy had been waving her frozen wand again to some effect that week and a string of meetings had to be abandoned.

Huntingdon announced they would inspect at 7.30 a.m. on the day of the race. Having done that and clearly determined to have racing if at all possible they decided they would inspect again at 11 a.m. The wives having decided to miss this one, Terry and self decided we would stick to our original plan and would leave for what is about a three hour journey at 10.30 a.m. On the way, we would stay in touch with the mid-morning inspection by mobile phone and radio bulletins.

As we drove east came the news that they would inspect again at one o'clock. Most of the track was raceable but there were a few stubborn frozen patches which, it was hoped, the sunshine would deal with.

As we drove into the racecourse we could see what looked like an army of people actually out on the track, every one them head bent as heels went into turf. As we walked into the owners' and trainers' came the news that nobody wanted. The meeting could not go ahead.

There was some grumbling – but we, like most people, seemed to have sympathy for the stewards. No matter which way they play it in these circumstances they can't win. All that said, we, like all the other owners, would be paying a bill for several hundred pounds because, of course, our horse had made the long journey to the track – and then gone all the way back again. Fortunately for us Gunner is a good traveller but for some horses it would have been an unpleasant – and pointless – experience.

As we made the long journey home I reflected that Huntingdon, which I had only visited for the first time in December, certainly didn't seem to be showing itself as one of my lucky tracks. The first visit had seen Burwood Breeze fall at the final fence …. the second visit featured the run out with Tony McCoy – and now this.

We consoled ourselves with the thought that at least we had a saver entry for Gunner at Chepstow on the Saturday and we thought we had a reasonable chance of getting in. That hope went down the pan after eleven o'clock on the Friday when he was balloted out. Not that it made much difference. Not too much later, the Chepstow meeting was abandoned because of snow – all of which produced more talk from me of stamp collecting being the chosen hobby when I was reincarnated next time around.

We settled on a northern expedition as being the best for his next outing, with a choice between Doncaster on the Saturday and a second preference entry at Market Rasen on the Sunday, depending on the ground. With just six still in at Doncaster and 16 at Market Rasen (you get the overnight declarations for both Saturday and Sunday racing on Friday) and the ground officially good at both places, it wasn't a hard decision.

Finding a jockey was another matter. We said to the Doc that we would be happy if either Mark Bradbourne or Jody Mogford were available. But there was racing at Newbury, Huntingdon and Kelso as well as Doncaster. A busy

Saturday really does stretch the jockey pool and you can see why the agents have become so important.

I was with a friend having coffee before joining Mrs B. at a restaurant when the mobile phone rang at 12.15 p.m. on Friday. Teresa was dealing with things because the Doc was in surgery. Unfortunately neither Jody nor Mark were available because of other riding commitments. Of the senior guys, the agents had told her Tom Scudamore and Jimmy McCarthy were available. Which one would we like?

After a conversation with Terry, we settled on Tom Scudamore.

I rang Teresa and thought that was that. Then at 12.45, just fifteen minutes before the one o'clock deadline by which trainers have to settle their riding arrangements or face a fine, Teresa rang again. Contrary to what she had been told earlier, neither of the two would take the ride. Could I please take over.

There then followed a frantic fifteen minutes as I tried to get in touch with the agents to sort it out – to no avail. In the end, at the 59th second of the 59th minute, we jocked David Crosse, the three pounds claimer, into the saddle. Quite what had gone on I am still not sure. Jimmy McCarthy had to do ten stones for a ride later at the same meeting and the word was that he needed to be in the sauna for several hours – but I can't say I was convinced.

I suspect that with Cheltenham looming neither man wanted to take risks in a novices race. Fair enough if that was the case – but equally fairly, I for one will remember next time round. Gunner had successfully got round Chepstow on his only outing over obstacles and I would have thought that the Doc's reputation (after all he rides in races against these guys) would have settled any worries about the safety of the ride.

'I thought', said my friend as we made our delayed way to the restaurant for lunch, and after all the phone to-ing and fro-ing, 'that you were supposed to have stopped having this kind of angst in your life'. Ah, I explained, this was pleasure angst - not business angst. When the dust settled Terry was succinct. As far as he was concerned, I could continue to be to be pole man for jockeys.

So for the first time this season we headed for the north country. Of course as a Geordie I am biased, but northern racing has a different atmosphere and people really are friendlier. As for Doncaster, while I fear the town will never make it as a holiday destination you would have to be pretty insensitive not to have some sense of history when you step on to the racecourse. They've been racing at Town Moor since the sixteenth century and it is home to the St Leger, the oldest of the flat classics.

There is a sense of occasion at the northern tracks which you don't get at many courses in the south of England. It's a proper day out and people dress up for it with more ties on show than you will see just about anywhere these days. The ladies, and particularly the younger ones, also make an effort. That, in the case of the younger ones, doesn't necessarily mean in the number of garments actually being worn.

This was a pleasant March day but with a wind which still had a touch of winter about it. Undeterred, many of the younger female racegoers had dispensed with coats ('they're just not fashionable, Dad' - according to my daughters) and were wearing outfits which depended to a remarkable degree on the combination of a neckline plunging to meet micro skirts which with equal velocity had shot up to remarkable heights. In the middle a wisp, no more, of this or that flimsy material.

They seemed totally unconcerned by temperatures which never went above 10C - although Mrs B. did confide that a visit to the ladies had produced the sight of some of these young women using the hand-dryers to try to get warm. Certainly around the racecourse they affected looks of complete insouciance – often in the face of stares from the male racegoers which were not entirely based on concern for their well-being. Meanwhile, back at the racing...

Doncaster is a dual-purpose course, staging both flat and jump racing. Certainly the ground staff know a thing or two about producing a tip-top surface to race on. The ground looked spot on and was, according to Terry, who had walked the course with Teresa, 'perfect jumping ground' – just what we wanted for our chap after the glue he had had to deal with on his hurdling debut at Chepstow.

We went into the weighing room with Teresa just as David Crosse was weighing out (as they'd arranged) and for Teresa to take his saddle. It gave us the chance for a few minutes' chat about the horse and what we could reasonably expect away from the sometimes snatched encounters you can get in the parade ring preliminaries.

The Doc was being a racecourse doctor for the day at Newbury but he had spoken to the jockey by phone. Terry and self made it clear that we fully expected Gunner to bring up the rear in a race where some of the horses had considerable experience both on the flat and over hurdles.

In fact there were a couple of pretty fancy young hurdlers in the race and we held our hands up and said our chap was there as part of his learning process. We wanted him to enjoy his race but learn some more about his business. David Crosse is another in the seemingly endless supply of young Irish horsemen who ply their tough trade this side of the water.

It was obvious he had fully taken on board the Doc's briefing and we came away not worrying about any sudden rushes of blood to the head by our rider which might give our horse the one thing we didn't want - a bad memory of the day.

David gave him just the ride we'd asked for - and we came as expected an undisgraced last, the extent of my hopes having been indicated in the £10 each way I had placed on him on the Tote.

'He's a really honest horse, he wanted to give me everything he had' said the jockey when he slipped out of the saddle. You can ask no more. Gunner had obviously been in a race and had picked up one tiny nick but was not in any way distressed. As consolation we take home £300 appearance money which will at least make a dent in the jockey and transport costs. And certainly Mr. Crosse goes on to our list of people we are more than happy to have aboard our youngster.

It is a bit of an odd process, taking the patient steps which an old-fashioned bred steeplechaser needs. But short of asking them to jump steeplechase fences straightway, there's not really another sensible road to travel. Needless to say, more races for NH bred horses would help. Anyway, one more outing and Gunner will at least have an official hurdling handicap rating.

Patience being our watchword, we shall give him a week or ten days to see how he comes out of the race before even thinking of forward plans. Meanwhile, I just hope that somebody upstairs is taking note of all this patience and practice of the Olympian virtues of 'taking part'. And of course, in the process, marking us down for future rewards.

Chapter
12

Robert Lester – Booming Bob

If you find bits of Bob Lester's story hard to believe, please don't worry. You are not alone. So does he.

Central to the whole story is, of course, Iris's Gift, stunning winner (having been second the previous year) of the Stayers' Hurdle at Cheltenham in 2004, taking the wind out of French sails by beating the mighty Baracouda. There then followed scenes in the winners' enclosure normally only associated with Irish success as Bob, landlord of the Red Cow in Nantwich in Cheshire, invited the entire crowd to come and help him drink the pub dry.

All that definitely happened, as did the horse's victory in the Martell Liverpool hurdle at Aintree in April and a second in the big stayers' hurdle at Punchestown a few weeks later. And what is also absolutely true (even if everybody, including Bob, has to pinch himself) is that he bought Iris's Gift out of field for £5,000. Many skilled and experienced horse people (including, whisper it, Terry Biddlecombe) had stood in the same field, shook their heads and turned down the then three-year-old.

The reason, says Bob, was not hard to see. 'He looked an ugly duckling, a real Dobbin. Great big head and long, gangly legs.' It is also true that he has turned down, at the last count, five separate offers of a million pounds plus for the horse. On the way, he was offered £80,000 after he won his first bumper at Worcester - and Bob was offered half a million pounds long before he won the Cheltenham Stayers'.

I've got a £30,000 car, we go to the Caribbean every year and there's money in the bank - what more do you want? If I sold him it would be like selling my mother. I don't care what I'm offered – he's not for sale at any price. And remember he's won over £300,000 already.

I have to say that when you meet Bob, as I did, in the bar of the Red Cow, that when he says something with real emphasis, you do tend to believe what he says.

Bob is completely bald and would easily pass to my eye for a very fit, recently retired Rugby League player whose face and ears have done their time in the scrum. Years of slinging sacks of coal on his back have left him with a physique which suggests you would be sensible not to push your luck. Then there's the voice. In tones which owe their allegiance unreservedly to south Manchester, he will never need a public address system. In fact, I suspect he could, if he wanted, be heard above all the other 64,999 cheering his horse home at Cheltenham or anywhere else.

'You know, we're the only pub in Nantwich that doesn't need a bouncer' he says in a musing rather than boastful way.

This bloke – and he is very definitely a bloke - is now 50. Born in Stockport, he left school at 16 and after a brief flirtation with engineering he soon followed his father and grandfather in the family coal business. Yes, he says, there had been horses in the coal business in his grandfather's time - but in his day it was strictly lorries. So any rumours that if Iris's Gift had been a failure as a racehorse he would have been pulling a coal wagon can also be put to one side.

Today, the excitement and amazement shines out of him - excitement at the success, amazement that it's happened to him. And you don't have to be with him long to work out that he can't quite believe it either.

Astonishing sums have been paid for geldings in the last few years, particularly so for a sport so inherently dangerous as jump racing. But Bob Lester is living his (and a lot of

(Right) Proud Robert Lester and daughter Megan lead in Iris's Gift and Barry Geraghty after winning the Cheltenham 2004 Bonusprint Stayers' Hurdle (Photos © Grossick Photography).

other people's) dreams. And what's more, he's enjoying every last second of it.

And he certainly warms the heart by proving wrong that cynical old adage that everybody has his price. Let's face it, if he was going to sell out, he would have done it by now.

There are two stories about how he paid for Iris's Gift – known as Ted - which he says are definitely not true. Number one that Bob paid for him out of the money left to him by his mother - the Iris in his horse's name: 'Absolute -----' and Bob uses the longer version of two words which mean the same thing and which both begin with a 'b' and end with an 's'.

She died just two weeks after the horse had been bought, mother not entirely convinced about the wisdom of the project. The horse was unnamed. A family conference was called to sort it out. Bob and his wife, Joanne, have five children, two boys and three girls, aged between 13 and 26. They came up with the name of Iris's Gift in memory of a much-loved mother and granny.

> But what is weird is that my mother had been trying for years to get compensation for my father, who had been a prisoner of war with the Japanese in Singapore. It came through about a fortnight after she died. Me and my sister got £5,000 each. This horse is eerie I tell you.

What is true is that Bob really does go to his mother's grave every time the horse runs and while he's arranging the flowers - irises of course - he tells her how the horse has done and what happens next.

The other story which has done the rounds is that Bob paid for the horse by selling some of the budgerigars he breeds. At the moment his budgies are being looked after by a friend in Devon ('He's been a mate and mentor for 30 years'). But soon they will be back in Bob's safe keeping. Plans are at an advanced stage for a new aviary at the back of the pub.

When I say he doesn't look like your average budgie breeder - not a subject on which I claim any real expertise - he very amiably points out that strong man Geoff Capes, all 29 stone of honed muscle of him, is a mate and a fellow breeder. Yes, he does make money from his budgies, but they didn't pay for the horse either.

> You've got to remember that a lot of people round here still use coal to heat their houses. When I sold my coal business a couple of years ago I was employing eight people full time. It was a successful business.

The Red Cow came out of the proceeds. 'The brewery say they've never known anybody turn round a pub so quickly. Mind you, the horse hasn't done us any harm. People come in just to shake my hand.' But watching the natural courtesy with which he handles both staff and customers and the way everyone is treated just the same, you can work out there is more to it than that. Being a natural showman, and definitely a personality, also help. And you can only suspect that the £1,000 round of drinks he bought the night he brought the trophy home from his big Cheltenham win will also have improved his profile in the locality. 'I was first to bed that night. Mind you, they had to carry me upstairs.'

Bob admits to being both a 'fun loving sort of guy' and 'a pints of beer bloke'. He clearly knows how to party - but as he sips a diet Coke at lunchtime with me and says he only drinks in the evening, the question about how many pints does he sink on an average night is one of the very few he declines to answer. The other two are the names of the people who've offered over a million for the horse ('That wouldn't be fair'); and what was wrong with Iris's Gift when he had 10 months off ('It was the vet who spotted the problem - but that's a secret between me, Jonjo and the vet').

But when you ask about the stroke of genius which allowed Bob to spot the potential of this horse where so

Bob Lester lifting the spoils, Cheltenham 2004 (Photo © Grossick Photography).

many others failed he's very straightforward. 'It was complete luck, one hundred per cent' says Bob without qualification. 'I just thought he was a bit of a character. But you could approach him He's as good as gold but when he's on the gallops or at the track he's got a bit of 'jack the lad' about him. He's saying 'I'll show you'.

'My coal yard was not two miles from his field and with Megan, my youngest, I used to go and feed him.' The field and attached stables are owned by the former jump jockey, Reg Crank. 'I used to deliver him coal and he would say "You should get back into it. Buy that grey horse."' Course what I didn't know was that he had offered the horse to just about everybody in Great Britain.'

Reg must have known he was interested. 'He was on the phone every night saying "Buy that horse, buy that horse." In the end, to shut him up, I did.' What may well have tipped the balance was Reg's sister in-law, Ann.

'She saw me looking at the horse one day and she came across and said "You should have that horse. He's the one for you."' She was suffering from cancer at the time. Now, thankfully, that's behind her and she's a regular in the fifty-odd band of family and friends who travel to see the horse run, no matter where. They, like Bob, make no secret in their delight in being connected with such a special horse.

It was from Reg Crank's yard that not only Iris's Gift has gone forth - but a few years earlier so too had Forest Gunner, winner of the 2004 Foxhunters at Aintree with Carrie Ford in the saddle. You may recall, Mrs Ford had prepared by giving birth to her first child just ten weeks previously.

Two hours earlier, at the same track, Iris's Gift had shown real fighting spirit to take the three mile hurdle in style. The connection between the two horses was in the breeding. Both came via Gunner B, the legendary National Hunt stallion.

Exciting stuff for us owners of Gunner B's (in the shape of the afore-mentioned Gloster Gunner) but it's not in truth the sort of breeding likely to set the heart of men like Jonjo O'Neill a-racing.

Bob Lester and Jonjo go back about twenty years, to the time when he was training in Cumbria and was battling with cancer with the same spirit and determination he had shown in his riding days. Bob had first got involved in racing thanks to a jockey who, in a long winter lay-off cause by the weather, took a job helping Bob deliver coal.

When the freeze-up ended, he invited Bob to see what he did. Soon Bob was hooked, travelling all over the

(Above) Iris's Gift winning at Cheltenham, Barry Geraghty (in plain yellow) on board.

(Photos © Grossick Photography).

199

country. Full or part ownership of three horses followed. They did nothing until along came Pearl Fisher who he sent to Jonjo on the jockey's recommendation. The horse ran second three times before winning twice in six days and, says his proud owner, 'I was drunk for a week'. There then followed a thirteen year gap.

He had sold his coal business and with his wife bought a 70-acre farm which they turned into a holiday complex. Things didn't go as well as they hoped. They sold up and he bought another coal business. 'But I always stayed in touch with Jonjo, seeing him at the races, having a chat. And sometimes I'd go and stay in Penrith.'

So when whatever urge possessed him to buy the big grey, it was to Jonjo he turned. He was no longer in his Cumbrian hideaway but instead installed as the boss in the £12 million racehorse paradise near Cheltenham called Jackdaws Castle. The whole venture was bankrolled by the legendary Irish gambler, owner and Manchester United shareholder, J.P. McManus (who is rumoured to be one of those who have tried to tempt Bob with folding money, large quantities of it, in exchange for his horse).

We can only speculate on what actually went through the trainer's head when his friend told him of his purchase and the background. Whatever it was, he told his friend to send the horse down and in three weeks he would be able to give an opinion. The options were: one, that he would be no good; two, to give him another year in a field; and three, perhaps give him some experience in point-to-points.

Within three days the great Irish jockey and trainer was back. They had worked the £5,000 bargain with an expensive animal owned by the same J.P. McManus. There was no doubt about which horse had been the more impressive. Johnjo said: 'He's not coming home. Sell no shares. If you do, I'll buy them all'. Iris's Gift was on his way. Three straight bumper wins left no doubt in anyone's mind that this horse was something special.

It would be hard to imagine a greater contrast between two men. On the one hand, the twinkly, tiny Irishman, soft-spoken and often very careful with his opinions, cards close to his chest. On the other, booming Bob, larger than life and about as open as they come.

But the respect is mutual. Bob says of O'Neill who he calls 'Boss': 'He's the best. You just have to see him with a horse to know, the way he runs his hands over them. It's something magical'.

With affection, O'Neill has described both horse and owner as being the same - nutcases who are both tough and full of character. And the trainer has made no secret of how highly he regards the horse. When that comes from a man who has sent so many good horses to the races and was the jockey who piloted Sea Pigeon, Night Nurse and Dawn Run to their greatest triumphs, that's saying something. And when he adds that Iris's Gift is the most exciting horse his yard has ever had, you have to listen.

> Jackie, Jonjo's wife, tells me how excited he is about my horse. She says they spend half the night with Jonjo saying 'This could be the one'. She also tells me - because of course he wouldn't - how much Jonjo appreciates how patient I was when we had the problem. She said other owners would have been on the phone all the time saying 'When's he going to run, when's he going to run'. To be honest, it never occurred to me to do that. I just wouldn't.

For Bob the success has already given him the time of his life. 'I'm loving every minute of it. It's great. We get invited to all sorts of do's, Jo and I, that we wouldn't have been invited to before and all because of the horse. But we know that and we enjoy ourselves.'

He says that there are a lot of people in National Hunt racing with their head up their (and here he describes an anatomically challenging position involving the rear end) – 'but there are plenty of really nice people as well'.

No matter what happens next, let alone what has already

happened, it will not top the experience for Bob and Jo of seeing their 20-year-old son, Christopher, pass out from the RAF. 'That was the best, the proudest moment' he says in a way which brooks no argument.

Nonetheless he is making horse plans for the future. He has two other chestnut Gunner B's plus Iris's Gift's half sister. And he is putting together a syndicate to race a Bob's Return mare. All will bear his mother's name so it could be that Iris's Dream, Iris's Prince or Iris's Princess will bring him further glory.

> I learnt the hard way. I won't be buying horses from the sales or from a seller. Buy them young and go on from there. And get a good trainer. Jonjo charges £45 a day and that's for the best facilities anywhere in the world for National Hunt racing. And remember he won't have more than a hundred horses in the yard. I reckon that with their turn-away time, it costs me £15,000 a year for Iris's Gift. It's worth it.

For the future, plans for Iris's Gift were are already made. After a holiday Iris's Gift will run for the first time over fences at Bob's local track at Bangor in a novice steeplechase. And despite what some bookie's ante post lists might tell you, there's never been any question of running the horse in the Sun Alliance Novices' Chase. Iris's Gift will go for the Gold Cup as a novice and try and topple Best Mate.

So it looks as if Bob will boom and Jim will hum. It will be some contest.

Oh yes … and then there's the horses.

Chapter 13

David's Diary 6

MARCH 27

There are 40 racecourses in England, Scotland and Wales where jumping currently takes place, 22 of them NH only and 18 dual purpose tracks. When I awoke this morning, I had been to 34 and had a runner at most of them. One thing at least about this day was sure. Before it was over that number would move to 35. Musselborough, Ayr, Cartmel, Towcester and Folkestone would remain for the moment unvisited – but Bangor beckoned.

There, after his last run at Ascot, Burwood Breeze was one of eleven due to go to post in the Tommy's Darts Beginners' Chase, a Class D over three miles and half a furlong and worth £8,000 in prize money. These are races for horses which have not previously won a steeplechase. Breeze, with his 17 runs without a win but six seconds to his credit certainly qualified.

It's a level weights contest and with no mares and all the geldings over six-years-old, we were all set to carry eleven stones two pounds apart of course from the horses ridden by conditionals and amateurs. There was a swings and roundabouts element to the race. The swing was in the shape of the horse which went off the 9/4 favourite, Valleymore. He's rated at 115 which meant that in a handicap we would have been receiving 18 pounds, the handicapper having dropped us one pound for the Ascot run (all contributions gratefully received). The roundabout came in the fact that along with one other runner, we would have been giving weight to all the rest.

On the question of jockeys, the one thing that was always clear was that we would not have Jason Maguire on board. A riding ban meant that he was having a short holiday.

Instead we have David Dennis, a fact which caused no concerns whatsoever. He knows Breeze well, having ridden him at both Cheltenham and Perth - the latter performance being one of the horse's best.

With Mrs Byrne visiting her Mum in Northumberland it was left to partner Terry to get me safely to Bangor. I could have had many worse co-drivers. He was born and brought up only a few miles from the track, a necessary qualification for finding your way easily through the maze of country lanes which have to be negotiated. This is the Bangor which is near Chester and not the one along the road from Colwyn Bay.

Trainer Tom was making the somewhat easier journey to Newbury and the plan had been that his wife Sophie would be with our horse. A 9 a.m. phone call put paid to that. Tom and Sophie's black lab, Molly, had started to give birth. Two pups had already found their way into the world when she rang. Would I mind awfully ... Of course I didn't, these things happen. And anyway, Alice who work-rides and looks after Breeze would be with him. Certainly there was no great mystery about the riding instructions. If he has a chance, go to the front between the second last and last - and not before. Remember McCoy!

Bangor is of course famous as the only racecourse in Britain which gets by without a grandstand. Now admittedly while I was there it did not rain on spectators or ground, which was officially good to soft, but there's no getting away from the fact that the grassy banks on which you stand to view the racing give you a terrific view. The other special feature is the head-on angle you get of the finish. I couldn't help noticing too that the run-in from the last has to be one of the shortest around, not necessarily a disadvantage when you have horse with a tendency to wonder what to do next when he finds himself in front.

Terry, who got to know the course over fifty years ago when he started racing with his Dad, says it's changed quite a bit over recent years. There might be no grandstand but it is neat and well organised and there is plenty of that mixture of country and town – tweed and tieless - which gives National Hunt racing its special flavour. We reckoned there must have been around three or four thousand people there and that's not unusual. Stand or no stand, the paying public seem to like the place.

It was 35 days since Breeze had made his last appearance in the somewhat different surroundings of Ascot. The suspicions of his jockey that day, James Davies, that he had a neck or back problem had proved well-founded. Treatment from the chiropractor, a couple of weeks of easy work and some special food supplement had him looking really well. He was running up rather light and his rest and extra food had done him no harm.

There was no escaping the fact that we had a real chance (how often have I written those words?). The somewhat embittered *Racing Post* Spotlight writer said: 'Runner-up in five of his last six completed starts (all in handicaps) and ought to have serious chances back in novice company here; has proved a real enemy to punters, however, beaten favourite on four of his last five starts and always likely to find a way of continuing to frustrate.' Well, I know how he feels.

After that, you couldn't be too surprised to discover that Spotlight went for another horse but I was glad to note that the same paper's Postdata and Topspeed had kept the faith along with the *Daily Telegraph*, *Independent*, *Daily Mail* and *Daily Mirror* who all named Breeze as their pick. I also knew that Tom had said he was working particularly nicely at home - and Alice who rides him every day told me he had never felt so well.

I had laid £300 at SP on credit and when Breeze was safely in the parade ring but before the jockeys arrived I had another £200 in the bookies' ring at 5/2 (his eventual SP). Out came David Dennis and after making sure he was happy with his riding instructions - Tom having rung him - we fell to discussing what Breeze had been up to since David had last ridden at Perth about ten months before. Amazing how so many of the jockeys have a very clear picture of Breeze running out at Huntingdon with Tony McCoy on board!

Then he was off to the start and Terry and self to the grassy banks. I can't say I felt particularly nervous at this point. It was when the loudspeaker announcement told us that Alice had won the £50 best turned out award that the butterflies began.

Delighted as I am for the stable staff, I am not alone in viewing such an award as the kiss of death. What would he do today? Honest, consistent and still - says his biased co-owner - with the best to come. But on the other hand, is he turning into what racing people call 'a character'– a talented horse who never quite delivers? And what's more, he's just won best turned out.

There was a delay while a horse was caught and remounted which did nothing for my nerves. For the first mile he was in the rear group; for the second, David moved him to mid-division; and then at the beginning of the third he was in the leading bunch. None of that caused the trembling in my hands which meant I was struggling to keep a steady view of the race through the binoculars. To this point, I had been lucky enough to be associated with twelve winners. Never before had the nerves done this.

What was causing my binoculars to literally shake was the ease with which our horse was running and jumping. As the others struggled, our chap never came out of a loping canter. And what's more the course commentator kept on pointing out that fact.

I wanted to tell him to be quiet. After all, the other jockeys and horses might hear.

Exactly as planned, with all the other jockeys hard at work, he took the lead just after the second last. I still couldn't believe how easily he was going. Normally, I love a good shout to help get my horses home but this time it was Terry who was roaring and I didn't dare let out even a strangled scream until he was safely clear of the final fence and easing away from the pursuers. After all the frustrations I had never dreamt he would record his first win so easily.

The next half hour passed in a whirl - presentations and pictures, kisses for Alice, pats for jockey David, and bear-hugs from a delighted Terry. You really do feel ten feet tall and of course this is what makes all the disappointments and frustrations worthwhile.

Of course it was a great shame Mrs Byrne wasn't there to share it. She had the right of veto as she couldn't be there. But she'd said no, let him take his chance.

We spoke on the phone immediately the race was over, the sixty-year-old daughter and the eighty-seven-year-old mother in their local bookies, Charlie Chisholm's, at Amble in Northumberland. Were there many there? I asked. 'It was packed.' Did they realise it was your horse? 'They did by the end.' What had her mother made of it? 'Well, she's not used to me jumping up and down and making quite that much noise in public.'

As well as a bottle of champagne and a cup (the first we've won) there will also be a cheque for £4,149. At the time, it's the last thing on your mind and in fact Mrs Byrne had to ring me back to ask what we'd won and then I'd had to look it up in the racecard.

It means that Breeze, with place money already of £3,300 in the bank, will have covered his costs for the season (which is not over yet). As for trainer Tom, I thanked and congratulated him when we spoke. His two runners at Newbury had produced a first and a third plus, of course,

Breeze's win. Not a bad day, I observed.

'And what's more' said Tom 'Molly has had ten puppies'.

APRIL 13

So there we stand, the three of us. Self, Mrs Byrne - and the chap with whom we started this adventure of owning racehorses eleven seasons ago. 'And how are you feeling - sick?' enquires our friend, himself the owner of a hurdler and two point-to-pointers all of whom have complex problems, seemingly split pretty well evenly between the physical and psychological.

The reason he asks the question is that we are about two minutes away from the start of the Letherby and Christopher Handicap 'Chase, a Class E over three miles for horses rated 0-110. The setting is appropriately Chepstow, the place where this diary began at the course's first jumps meeting of the season at the beginning of October. This will be last jumping session of this season and there'll be one more National Hunt day in early May before the flat boys take over towards the end of the month.

I think only fellow owners can fully appreciate the extraordinary cocktail of emotions you feel at this moment, a unique mixture of adrenalin, hope, dread and fear. 'Do you think everybody feels the same?' asks our friend. There's just time, as the runners including Burwood Breeze circle at the start, to explain that in recent weeks I have asked roughly that question of the five other owners who feature in this book. They have all confirmed that emphatically they do.

Indeed, Alan Lee, *The Times* racing correspondent, created a wonderful image of one of them, the completely-bald Bob Lester, the owner of Iris's Gift, after his horse had won at Aintree. 'Entering the winners' enclosure, Lester yelled to no-one in particular: 'Why do I do this? It's why I've got no hair.'

With or without hair, male or female, young or old, I think the vast majority of owners can well understand the sentiment.

Part of today's cocktail has been created by two different elements. In partner Terry's absence (in Scotland on holiday – how dare he when he's needed) I have done my own detailed look at the other 10 runners in the field. What normally happens is that having taken a pretty good look at the form, I take a view and then discuss it with Terry who has done the really seriously scientific stuff.

In his absence I have been forced to do the detail myself. After many hours I have formed the very definite view that we have an A1 chance, not least because so many of the others are out of form whereas, of course, our last run at Bangor means there is a figure one immediately next to Breeze's name. This plus the fact that the form tells me all the realistic opposition need far greater cut in the ground than today's officially good conditions will offer.

So when, a couple of hours before our race, we bump into Terry Warner, Rooster Booster's owner, and he says he reckons our horse has a squeak but that he fancies two others more, I take a more robust view than I would normally when faced with such a long-term student of form. I give my reasons and report that our fellow is reported to be in 'terrific form at home'. Even Terry's realistic riposte 'Whatever that means' does not dent my confidence and I head off to what we must now call totesport (the Tote Credit Club as was) and once there, with Mrs Byrne, have to make a choice.

We find Burwood Breeze is on offer as the 4/1 favourite. The Press Association has him at 5/1 favourite and the *Racing Post* also favourite at 11/2. That paper's Spotlight correspondent is less than enthusiastic. 'Didn't have to improve to win a race where market leaders were below their best at Bangor but raised 7lb for that success so more to do in handicap company.' Meanwhile the chancers who write the editorial for the racecards have been sticking their necks out again. In his eight runs up to today in this season Breeze has won once, been second four times and third

Breaking his duck – Burwood Breeze with jockey David Dennis is led in by work-rider Alice after his first win at Bangor.

Trainer Tom's wife -
Sophie George with
Burwood Breeze.

once. This has provoked the risky comment: 'Live
contender today, solid each-way claims'.

With the nearest contender to Breeze offered at 7/1 and
drifting in totesport, the clear implication of the market is
that there has been money for him. I, of course, have got this
decision wrong before, taking an early price only to see SP
the better option. But today, in explaining the choice to Mrs
Byrne, I decide to take the 4/1 price - as does she.

Our visit to the pre-saddling area and the parade ring go
to make up another element of the cocktail referred to
earlier (the 'hope' element). Neither visit does do anything
to dent my confidence – quite the reverse in fact. Trainer
Tom and stable hand Alice both confirm our horse's well-
being at home and, says Tom 'I have never known him to
be better'.

In the parade ring it becomes clear that both Tom and
jockey Jason ('It's nice to be riding him again at last') really
do think he is going to add to their winners' tally. In fact,
good professionals though they are, it is obvious that both

211

are a bit more keyed up than normal. The statistics tell us why.

Season's end is only a couple of weeks away when league tables will be studied and reputations enhanced or diminished. Both are desperate to crack the 50 winners mark for the first time. As we speak, Tom is on 48 having had two winners in the last 24 hours. Jason rode both of those bringing his tally to 46.★★ They have four horses running at the Cheltenham two-day meeting which begins the next day – 'but you don't count those in your possibles the way you do with horses like Breeze in a race like this' explains Tom.

Their confidence settles it and I decide to punt the maximum I had settled on in advance. I lay another £150 to win by phone, this time at 7/2 and head off to the bookies' ring. The decision to take the early price is immediately confirmed as the right one–faced as I am with a sea of boards all offering Breeze as the 3\1 favourite.

There then follow a few moments of pure farce. Mid-way down the front rank I spot a board offering him at 100/30. Thinking nothing of the fact that this bookie looks much fitter than the average, I hand over my £100 bet at that price and look round to try and find similar or better. I see 7/2 at the bottom of the second row and head for it – but who's just ahead of me? Why, it's the 100\30 bookie. He obviously lays off my bet and the 7/2 bookie wipes the price. But look over there – there's one more board offering 7/2. Going into full 16-stone sprint mode I head off only to be beaten again by a short-head by the whippet-like bookie. Again as I thrust £100 in notes the price is wiped. 'Ah hell and I'm the owner' says I.

Past experience has taught me that a stone face which would make a sphinx look animated usually follows such

★★ Tom made it – Jason just failed. Tom's half century (his previous best in a season was 28) came with his very last runner of the season at Perth, appropriately enough with J.M.Maguire in the saddle.

remarks. I have complained elsewhere about the way many ring bookmakers ignore the orderly queue of ordinary punters in front of them and accept a big lay-off bet shouted at them from one of their of own brotherhood. They then wipe the price and refuse the bets of those who have waited in line.

But thank goodness there are exceptions to every rule. This bookie smiles and says in as pleasant a manner as you could imagine 'In that case sir, it's a pleasure to lay your bet'. You get a warm glow after this kind of experience and for a few moments the immediate prospects of the race were forgotten as I headed off to find Mrs Byrne - talking as I have described to our original horse-racing partner - which is where in this chapter you came in.

We stand in bright spring sunshine on the grass lawn in the members' enclosure having forsaken the impossible crush in the bar in owners'and trainers'which stops you getting either to or from the recently built viewing area.

Today - is this the first time at Chepstow? - we have the benefit of a big screen which allows us and everyone else to follow the bits of the race which otherwise happen out of sight as the horses round the bottom bend and head up the hill.

We've agreed in advance that Breeze will be ridden in the back half of the 12 runners for the first circuit and then move him through. For the first half mile the race is run at a very slow pace. 'Does this suit him?' asks our friend. The answer is not really - Breeze is not famous for his finishing kick. But then some pace is injected and everyone settles down, the riders of the leading half dozen able to stop taking a tug to prevent their horses going into the lead.

Mrs Byrne starts to fret with Breeze settled among the back four or five but with a mile to run Jason smoothly takes him up to the front four. Breeze hits the fourth last and is caught flat-footed as a result as the other leaders quicken. I thought our chance was gone. But no, the horse

At full stretch over the water - our first winner, Secretary of State.

who has never looked entirely sure about what he should do in a tight-fought finish this time battles gamely under Jason's driving.

As they came to the last he is back in with a shout. The *Racing Post* reported 'A cracking finish to this average handicap ... Burwood Breeze had more to do than when scoring at Bangor last time and his good effort suggests he is still progressing. He had to work hard to get in a blow but responded gamely to pressure and a better jump at the last might have seem him prevail.'

In fact he pecked on landing at the last and for a split second I thought, as nose headed towards turf, that he was going to fall. He didn't. Jason, who had stayed 'neat' gathered him up and gave the winner a run to the line. In truth I knew we were booked for second place on the run-in. All credit to the length and a half winner, Felix Darby, a nine-year-old winning for the first time and running from five pounds out of the handicap. I made sure I said as much to his naturally delighted winning owner.

As we headed for second place in the winners' enclosure our friend made two points. One, we were giving the winner a stone and a half; and two, the second prize of £1,200 was considerably more than he'd got for some of his winners.

All true, but there was no getting round the fact that there was an air of disappointment from owners, trainer and jockey. 'We have had a lot of coming second with this fellow' said Tom; while Jason observed 'If only we'd jumped the last'.

With form figures in the period covered by this diary (the full year's figures plus costs can be found in Chapter 14 'Totting Up') of 213RO22F and winnings of around £8,000, there are a lot of owners out there who would be offering right arms to be in this position - but it's hard not to feel this is a horse not quite fulfilling his potential.

The decision about who should ride the horse had not been straightforward. It's not easy to by-pass a jockey who has ridden a horse well into first place and in the case of David Dennis had also got perhaps the best run ever from him at Perth. On the other hand, Jason had done virtually all his schooling and been second on him three times. Tom had left it to me - and I had opted for Jason.

And of course after a race like this you wonder. My conclusion, as I said to Mrs Byrne, was that I feel David gets the horse to jump better. Jason is stronger and he had got a fighting finish out of him - which is important for the future - and kept the partnership intact to do it. It's an impossible dilemma to resolve.

With Breeze looking so well, another run - provided he comes out of this race o.k. - is very much on the cards.

As for his owners, it took - as it does, win or lose - a few hours for the cocktail to subside. And of course like true addicts, we'll be back. What is it they say about alcoholics? One drink is too many and a thousand not enough.

Chapter
14

Totting Up – and some questions

Right at the beginning of this book, I highlighted one of the questions you are always being asked as an owner 'Do you make any money at it?' Well, as promised, here are the facts and figures for the four horses who figure in these pages, for the whole National Hunt season, end April 2003 to April 2004.

For comparison, you will also find the average costs for NH owners and flat owners from the latest figures as published by the Racehorse Owners' Association in autumn 2003. Please note that the ROA have included insurance costs. The reason for the difference between NH and flat insurance costs is simply that jump racing is more dangerous. Because of the cost of insurance premiums we do not insure our horses.

The ROA figures presume that all owners recover their VAT (which we do); that no sponsorship income is included; that training costs are payable for the full 12 months of the years; and that farrier and vet's bills are for routine costs.

With my own figures, they are based on what was actually paid and won. We do not keep them with trainers when they are not racing.

BURWOOD BREEZE (100%owned)
Number of runs   10
Wins 1 /Seconds 5/ Thirds 1/Fourths nil

Training costs (inc. vets, farrier & jockeys) £9,314
Racing and transport costs £1,714
Registration charges £154
Entry fees £985
Total costs £12,167

Prize money £10,540
(after trainer and jockey deductions)

Profit/Loss Loss £1,627
(15.5%)
Cost recovery 85.5%

So we made the frame 70% of the times he ran which at ten outings was nearly three times the average for jumpers. The costs are also an awful lot better than average. If you can get near covering the running costs (ignoring, of course, the cost of buying the horse which in this case was £15,000) you are doing pretty well.

KLONDIKE CHARGER (100% owned)
Number of Runs 12
Wins 2/ Seconds 1/ Thirds 5/ Fourths nil

Training Costs (inc. vets, farrier & jockeys) £6,639
Racing and transport costs £1,310
Registration costs £154
Entry fees £704
Total cost £8,807

Prize money
(after trainer and jockey deductions) £10,469

Profit/ Loss Profit £1,662
(19%)
Cost recovery 119%

A 66% record for making the frame – a minor miracle, as are the figures (in fact in that area, forget the 'minor'). The horse cost £6,000 so he has not only covered his running expenses but made inroads into the capital outlay. Interesting to note how many times he ran, 12, compared to the average of 3.5 a season. Credit to horse and trainer. Also, despite the fact he won two chases, if we hadn't had all those second and third places we would have gone into the red.

JESSIE MACDOUGALL (50% owned)
Number of Runs   8
Wins Nil /Seconds Nil/Thirds 1/Fourths 3

Training Costs (inc vets, farriers & jockeys) £6,212
Racing and transport costs   £619
Registration charges   £154
Entry fees   £565
Total costs   £7,550

Prize money   £1,742
(after trainer and jockey deductions)

Profit/loss   Loss £5,808
                                            (77%)
Cost recovery   33%

Nearly double the average cost recovery for jumping owners and she did have a 50% strike rate in getting us into the winners' enclosure. She remains the 'what might have been' of our racing year. As she was 50% owned, half of the loss, £2,904, needs to go into our final figures for the season.

GLOSTER GUNNER (50% owned)
Number of runs   4
Wins Nil/ Seconds Nil/ Thirds Nil/ Fourths Nil

Training Costs (inc vets, farriers & jockeys) £5,222
Racing and transport costs   £360
Registration charges   £154
Entry fees   £159
Total cost   £5,895

Prize money
(after trainer and jockey deductions
from appearance fee)   £243

Profit/loss   Loss £5,652
                                             (95%)
Cost recovery   5%

Pretty grim reading. Gunner, for all his charms, will have to show us something next season to justify continuing. Again, because he is 50% owned, half the loss – £2,826 – goes in to the final figures.

So for the year recorded in the diary the total cost of running the four horses (two 50% owned) was £27,696

Owners prize money (50% in 2 cases)   £22,001
Loss   £5,695
                      Cost recovery around 80%

So it cost us £5,695. In return our horses ran 32 times at 19 different tracks and we travelled around 7,000 miles to see three winners, 6 seconds and 7 thirds.

It is for others to say. But I'm with Joe in Dickens's *Great Expectations* when he said to the main character Pip **'What Larks'**.

Average annual cost of National Hunt racehorse ownership

Training   £12,000
Racing and transport costs

(average 3.5 runs)	£1,190
Insurance	£1,000
Registration charges	£270
Entry fees	£316
Total average annual cost	£14,776
Prize money	
(after trainer/jockey deductions)	£2,745
Average annual loss	£12,031
Cost recovery	18.6%

Average annual cost of Flat racehorse ownership

Training	£14,200
Racing and transport costs	
(average 5.5 runs)	£1,733
Insurance	£550
Registration charges	£320
Entry fees	£1,035
Total average annual cost	£17,838
Prize money	
(after trainer/jockey deductions)	£4,980
Average annual cost	£12,858
Cost recovery	27.9%

One interesting sidelight on the whole money question. Dr. Philip Pritchard, one of our trainers and very much a central character in this book, who has both Klondike Charger and Gloster Gunner in his care, runs his 16-horse string under the slogan 'Affordable Fun'. At less than £150 basic a week the Doc is certainly not overcharging and he is proud of the fact that in the season under review his owners were showing cost returns of around 60 per cent.

The Doc is quite shameless in trying to find new ways of justifying that slogan. He likes nothing better than keeping an eagle eye on entries and coming across a race with handsome prize money – preferably down to sixth place- and with hardly any entries. It may mean horses being hugely over-faced but if they can get amongst the prize money, the Doc says 'so what?'

He is, too, a great exploiter of the appearance money scheme. Sometimes people smile in a condescending manner about his efforts - but when you pop along on a Sunday morning and see the range of people enjoying racehorse ownership you might well ask who is doing racing the greatest service.

To go from the very particular to the worldwide, there has been an improvement for British owners in their returns, according to the latest figures from the International Federation of Horseracing Authorities and revealed in the *Racing Post* in August last year. That average return (for both flat and NH owners) quoted from ROA figures in Chapter 1 of about a quarter of costs recovered was about 10 per cent up on figures two years previously.

But don't get too excited. That still leaves Britain joint 35th in the worldwide table of forty countries surveyed, alongside Austria. For Irish owners, there's been an improvement to 32 per cent of costs recovered, while in France the figure is now 55 per cent.

Of course 'Do you make money?' is by no means the only question. The related one is: 'Will you let me know when your horse is going to win?'

I think I can only answer that question by asking one myself. Are you sure you've read my diary?

Another frequent query - and it's not been a great year to be asked - 'Is racing straight?' Like many others, and despite what has happened and is being investigated, I believe that fundamentally it is, otherwise why continue to put money into what you know to be a crooked charade. But obviously there are some funny folk about.

As long as there is big money involved you will always get people who will try it on and clearly the Jockey Club security operation - now in very different hands - has in the past not been as worldly as it might.

Betting exchanges, where punters can be either backers or layers, have brought a whole new dimension to racing gambling. I never doubted that it was sensible that owners should be among the people forbidden to bet against their own horses.

Of course getting technological genies back into bottles is pretty well impossible and in one form or another the exchanges are here to stay. But as well as running clean ships, ways must also be found for the exchanges to make a proper contribution to the cost of the sport.

I thought Peter Savill, the then British Horseracing Board chairman, made a telling point in October 2003 when he said he estimated the betting exchanges were responsible for a £20 million drop in racing revenues. Why? Because for every £1billion placed in betting shops, racing gets £14 million. And for every £1 billion bet on credit or on the internet racing receives £7million. But he said that the BHB estimated that for every £1 billion matched on the exchanges, racing receives only around £1 million.

And so, what about the future? Well for sure, wife and self will continue to be involved.

Burwood Breeze has been a model of consistency and effort as well as adaptable in terms of going - but also the cause of a degree of frustration. Several of the season's seconds could so easily have been wins and then what a season it would then have been. The horse has so many of the right attributes but if only we could add a dash of finishing speed and a hint of fighting spirit to the existing mix.

The other obvious problem is that - God bless him - he keeps running up to his handicap mark. He finished the season on his best ever mark of 104 and with a top RPR rating of 111 and that's where he'll start the new season. I don't think we can complain but it doesn't help.

He will be nine come the New Year, prime time in the life of a staying 'chaser. I will be keen next time around to try him at some of the tracks which offer a stiffer test of jumping - the likes of Sandown, Cheltenham, Ascot and - dare I say it - Huntingdon.

But all that said, you can't but be pleased with a horse which has almost paid his way and got us into the winners' enclosure as often as he has. And what's more shown an ability to cope with anything from soft to good to firm. That's meant that one of his owners has spent rather less time than he would otherwise worrying about something as unreliable as the British weather.

Klondike Charger is now officially ten and about 110 in the ways of the world. He goes into his new season of summer jumping off a mark of 88, that's just one pound more than he was before the first of his two wins at Fontwell in August 2003.

We shall start him off at Stratford and then aim him towards the twists and turns of Fontwell once more. There are really only a few of the tracks you can take him to. Fakenham may well be worth a go and Sedgefield is a possibility - but wife and self will somehow have to blot out the downpour which greeted our arrival there last time and which did for Colin's chances long before the off.

We have had several expressions of interest for him as a point-to-pointer. Being sensible we shall have to think about it, depending how the season goes. Touching wood as I write it, he has never fallen in 38 outings over obstacles so you can see why he could do well in the point-to-point field. That plus a fact which will certainly suit the old rascal- they go slower between the flags.

Gloster Gunner has things to prove. He has undoubtedly grown and strengthened and certainly has shown promise jumping steeplechase fences. But does he want to be a racehorse? Certainly the bare statistics would test the faith of anyone.

He has now had four outings – one bumper, two hurdles and a steeplechase. He has finished last in all four, although admittedly two failed to finish in two of his races. The only rating he has received so far is a *Racing Post* Top Speed rating of - wait for it - 11. Not quite what we had hoped - and continue to hope - for.

Trainer and joint owners all agree that he will have to show something once he's fit in the new season to keep the dream alive. If it does not work out on the race track, the good news for Gunner is that his handsome build and good paces have attracted interest from people who know in the eventing world. And his genuine good nature and willing heart will make him popular wherever he goes.

But nobody has given up hope. Some time off and some more strengthening could well do the trick. Let's hope so, because Four for Fun took a bruising when Jessie MacDougall broke down at Cheltenham and, even if I say so myself, we have earned some better luck.

If we do sell Colin, and Gunner should fail to make the grade, we will aim to replace them. I have bought horses at the sales, out of trainers' yards and bred them - but I have never bought a horse at the races in either a seller or a claiming race. Perhaps that will be a way to travel next time.

Of course no matter how we do it, rattling around in my head will be Mr. Lester's £5,000 purchase not to mention the cost of a couple of other of my Cheltenham heroes. Did you know that Champion Hurdler, Istabraq, cost less than £40,000? Or that Gold Cup winner, See More Business, was less than £6,000?

Yes, yes … But remember the alternative title for this book was 'Madness I know …'.

Now as we began with some quotations, I see no good reason not to end with one. Please never forget the hold horses have over many of us.

Rudyard Kipling, no less, put it far better than I ever will:

> *Four things greater than all things are,*
> *Women and horses and power and war*

Chapter 15

Postscript

In a dizzying eight days in May, we ran Klondike Charger three times as he started his new season. He surprised everyone – including, I suspect, himself – by finishing fourth while over a stone out of the handicap in a Class C 'chase over an extended two miles at Stratford on the Saturday. We had seen it as a pipe-opener to get his season under way before tackling the longer distances.

Delighted as I was, my worst fears were realised when the handicapper stuck him up six pounds for that effort. But the horse was in such a good mood I pressed to send him to Fontwell just four days later, where we had a back-up entry over two and a quarter miles.

He won by five lengths at 4/1, cruising home for his fourth win in seven outings at the West Sussex track. With Andrew Thornton out because of an elbow injury, James Davies had the ride at both Stratford and Fontwell, getting some great jumps out of our chap.

And it was James in the saddle again on the Sunday, when he set forth over two and three quarter miles once more at Fontwell. He had to bear top weight this time and it was just too much – but he ran a highly creditable fourth, beaten 10 lengths by a horse carrying over one and a half stones less.

Colin had added nearly £5,000 to his winnings. And in the process he really had paid for himself as I had originally hoped in November and realised I'd got wrong when I did the end of season tot. And what a week we had. For whatever reason, Colin really looked to be enjoying his racing and his owners certainly enjoyed themselves.

Don't worry – we won't keep running him at that rate. But with him in the right mood and no more Fontwell for a couple of months, it was too good a chance to miss.

We also ran Burwood Breeze three times more before the end of May and calling a halt to his campaign. He added £6,000 to our winnings with runs at Kelso, Perth and Stratford.

Where did he finish? He was second of course.

Three times.